PASSCHENDAELE AND THE SOMME

PASSCHENDAELE
AND
THE SOMME

A DIARY OF 1917

BY

HUGH QUIGLEY

First Published in 1928

Printed and bound by Antony Rowe Ltd, Eastbourne

NOTE

The diary, as written in 1917, has been reproduced without modification. It was my intention at first to issue it anonymously, but the possibility of critics doubting its authenticity made this course inadvisable. The diary owes nothing to later inspiration, and remains as it was composed on the dates and at the places mentioned. A slight regrouping to preserve some form of emotional or narrative sequence may have broken up strict chronological sequence here and there. The preface as written in 1918 has been retained, since its spirit is that of the diary. In France, during the period in question, I served with the 12th Royal Scots in the 9th Division.

H. Q.

LONDON, S.W.15
January 1928

PREFACE

(WRITTEN IN 1918)

I venture to think the following letters are quite distinct from the bare-backed narration of the usual war correspondent. They were written in the summer and autumn of 1917, a year of great struggle and greater sacrifice, when the issues came home more vividly to the mind and confronted one with immense possibilities, the substance of life and the pre-eminence of death, to a greater extent than in the preceding years. I might argue this in extenuation for the purely psychological character of those letters: perhaps I was mistaken in the atmosphere, perhaps too much absorbed in self to note any real difference in the mental " milieu," but I thought, and still think, in spite of any consideration put forward by critics, that the feelings expressed in those letters represented to a very great degree the general feelings of my comrades-in-arms.

To this must be added that in no case have I applied verbal ornamentation or arabesque at any subsequent date : the letters remain as they were written at the time. The only retouching consisted in omitting purely private passages. This desire for local truth would not permit me to chisel and polish : I preferred to let them remain as they are—rude, exaggerated, over-tense in places, too lyrical, perhaps—the record of one who tried, to the best of his power, to reconstruct that time of emotional stress and unequalled difficulty of retaining mental stability, not by bald enumeration of gross detail, but by an expression of subtle things, essentialized from things seen, from agonies felt.

Hence, as a picture of war in France during the summer and autumn of 1917, this collection must remain very unsatisfactory indeed ; no raids, no spectacular battles, no display of super-conceited bravery as Ian Hay describes, no minute progression as we find in Philip Gibbs, but rather a journal of emotion striving to make emotion essentialized the centre of all, the ultimate criterion of all. Perhaps, a novelist looking for motif might find a little material in them : the historian will certainly find none.

Of that I am quite legitimately proud, and even if my conception of life does not coincide with the conventional, even if I lay too much stress on the ego, even if I have the French peculiarity of becoming too preoccupied with soul and heart, yet I shall always feel thankful that this confession will remain a mirror to me of the agony of that time, poignant, perhaps, but beautiful in recollection. A memory of trial and sacrifice, yet a memory of great beauty caught by an awakened spirit and subtilized to life itself !

Just now, when I may have forgotten the mud of Flanders, I have certainly not forgotten the despairs and sudden illuminations of the spirit, the agonies and rejoicings of the heart itself. To most the war will remain that—an emotional memory, a confession of great adventure hazed in a great glow of spirit.

Perhaps, when we have outgrown this time and reached the tranquil stage, when

Passchendaele will have become indeterminate history preserved in memoirs, the writer might arise who could resuscitate those emotions for us and, scorning ephemeral overloaded detail, trace truly and nobly the vibrations of a soul to the horrors and beauties of this war, the faint impressions of the spirit become tangible at last, and a definite part of life.

H. Q.

LANARK,
May 1918

CONTENTS

		PAGE
PREFACE	. . . .	vii
I. FROM THE BASE TO BILLETS NEAR ARRAS	.	1
II. THE SOMME	. . . . . .	51
III. FLANDERS	. . . .	103
IV. FLANDERS (*continued*)	. . . . .	143
A DEATH IN HOSPITAL	. . . .	186
INDEX	. . . .	189

PASSCHENDAELE AND THE SOMME

I

FROM THE BASE TO BILLETS NEAR ARRAS

Folkestone,
20 June, 1917

At sunset we passed by the Lake, where I can only remember a village sunk in a hollow and a red fire spreading over indefinite shadows of hill. Lying on the carriage floor I fell asleep, and awakened with a start to a cry that the sea lay near and our destination. A sleepy fool had mistaken the broad Thames for the ocean : in the light of a drear grey dawn I saw it, with its lighters grouped like cattle under the sun, and a shadow stealing across the water of Westminster, tenuous as the air. We went by Wandsworth Road, Battersea, skirting lifeless clumps of architecture, and in Kent occasional fields of hops, long and graceful round their poles.

Morn was a maiden shrouded in mist when we stopped at Ashford. There was no indication that her face would be a sunny smile, prelude to peaceful laughter, or a mournful dropping of tears. Our leader marched us off to Folkestone Rest Camp, where we stayed the day.

I can yet feel the great peace of that cluster of hotels, framed in noble elms, something that stole like a shy benefactor into the heart, and, while breathing a lovely faith in life and a fair dawn, would not disclose her name or break her silence. A perfect beauty of clear air and clear sky, rich to a promise; in the blue an airship was hovering, and the thrush was throwing, head back, her full song to the day. I had heard of the quiet glory of old English towns, but this surpassed all conception. Brooding of slaughter in trenches, and wounds, and shell explosions; brooding that lead the soul to the great darkness and buried it in the labyrinth where no hope gleams and the heart sinks down to an agony of misery beyond dream and outside human conception; brooding of useless hopes, died away to a chaste, pure note of trust, a solemn faith in the great destiny. Henceforth I can view a time of struggle on the battlefield with equanimity, for I know the ultimate beauty is good, and all this striving, ideal endeavour. I have no need of internal inspiration, for I have renewed my own creed and strengthened my soul against trial.

I spent an hour of pure interest watching the soldiers walking up and down, kilted, breeched, and in trousers : all regiments of the Army, and all departments. Every man exulted in the hope of seeing loved ones again, and when the soiled, weary, overburdened procession passed away I comforted myself with the thought that perhaps one day I should know that pleasure and taste that exquisite delight.

ETAPLES,
26 June, 1917

The ceaseless tread of feet moving to a leaden march, when can I forget it and bring a new life to my anguish ; when can I silently drink in the immortal splendour of an emerald land. Night and day I hear them, the helmeted, heart-sick warriors, bowed beneath a load of baggage and straps, doubled by the greatest load of all ; I cannot cast them aside and bury myself again in a gracious dream. No courage rests in my heart, and my thought, tired with overwork, turns on itself and rends the soul with sick foreboding. I have a fugitive glance of green poplars, plated with gold in the sun, and brown sails creeping down a river to a white sea ; the airs of a clear sky fly round me, and there is a distant sobbing on the dunes. O God! If that were so! If I could steal forth and gather up those beauties like Ceres in the wheat, and bring them to a rich fruit in living image and merry point, gay jest and happy gurgle of a choice delight! But the marching feet trample down my flowers and there is no gain save in an agony of repining.

I have made a brave effort to conquer an invincible loathing and grow excited in work which could not foster my soul's development. Bombing, I pretended, was good fun, and the essence of romance lay in sleeping under canvas on dirty boards and gazing the live-long day on a rayed roof. But the prison seals everything, sears every fresh budding to dry torment. It brings the eternal autumn ; its colour is brown and dark purple—purple of despair and brown of shadow.

No books interest me : even Dante escapes

my reason, and I find no meaning in the jewelled words. I have no heart for anything, but stupor overcomes me and I long for the end, for the time when I may walk under the whispering trees, beside cool waters, over the wet grass, hear the thrush on his high perch, and trace the crimson cloud wandering to eve. Immortality rests a dubious reward for striving, and eternal light a poor compromise for present darkness. Every soul has its purgatory ; I have had mine, and no longer can I hope to breathe the celestial peace. Religion gleams but poorly, and falsity rings through its utterance, like a lady pitching music too high for the breast. Moodily the home comes to me : strawberries will be red-cheeked and the berries pendulous under leaves, the garden riot in flowers and the wild rose clamber beside weedy brooks, heavy the dark shade of the sycamores and turquoise the hanging cloud on the moors. I have lived all that ; that was my very life, the whole of me, the centre of my happiness. That was my God, the symbol of a great faith and noble trust. Now they are taken away, what remains ? Nothing but a moping round tents in the white glare of sun or sand, a life in death, a useless cognizance of thwarted hopes.

ETAPLES,
27 June, 1917

I can feel a clarion-call ringing within, a call that brings my mood to the skies and enchants me with hope. A moment of great ecstasy, like a first enraptured answer to the eternal caress ! There appears no reason for it, just a gathering together of the vital forces to throw off gloom and leap boyishly into happiness. It comes like the wind, and will pass like it, leaving a clear and purified air. With its exaltation my outlook gleams rose ; hope is a near angel laughing at me from behind a cloud, and I would dare anything, face anything, knowing the hand stays by me and the presence glides by me still. A rebirth of sweet longing passion, when the past misery falls off and the perfect being emerges, bright-eyed in the future dawn. Would it could last thus for ever, and accompany me to the last sleep ! I feel superior to all ; laughter bubbles forth from a joyous heart and the sympathy becomes real and palpitating. I have such pride in my new possession that I can look at my comrades-in-arms, dust-wrinkled and swarthy, with the note of condescension, glad that this precious gift remains mine, and that this gleam rests on the road before me and softens the white glare. I am almost happy, alone, isolated, nursing my own quiet enthusiasm, self-contained for once, beyond the need of companion. The elemental rises and the overcultured lapses back into a memory, a listless effort of will. No need for inspiration from without ; my body is my own poem— life, a glorious pæan, like the singing of birds in the shadowy dunes and the subdued whisper of a broken wave on shore.

All day the mood has stirred me, and now that the woods grow heavy with blue shadow against a golden sea, where the fishing-boats fly a sail or two and lie dotted along the crests of the trees, and the sky blooms a delicate primrose, the memory goes back on what it felt and lives anew the delicate happiness.

The artist in me awoke at last, spontaneously like a flood, raised the depressing monotony of tent and put into a lovely harmony the peacock-blue and snow-white. I lay on my back in the warm air of the tent, gazing through the half-open flap at the sandy road before. The flap glowed dark grey with an indistinct silhouette of khaki leaning against it smoking a pipe : beyond blazed the white, deeply-dented path trod by figures almost white themselves, bearing away a deep-blue shadow and melting ghost-like into the shimmer. I could not see the tent's edge against the fiery sky; there was no beginning and no end to tell where the white cloth projected against the pale sapphire. The glare had grown so intense that only shadow made a definite record, deep indigo within and a boot or two rising into light, a box-edge and a gleaming mess-tin coruscated with jewels of fire. I thought of Egypt, and placed myself on the desert under a great sun; if I could paint only shadow and let the rest be imagined, there would be a lovely combination of pale grey-green of uniform, pale cobalt of shimmering sky, snow-white of tent, and deep blue of shadow. That would remain all, no definite contour of ruddy face and grey eye and round cheek, but an invisible group of colour brought to life by shadow alone. The poem of a white heat!

After all, I can say I have struggled with depression, like Laocoon in the toils, fought against the shadowy evil that drags my soul into darkness and extinguishes all gleaming, risen above him and fluttered a new wing. If the agony is great, how great the ecstasy! My life appears like a ploughed field, one day on the crest, another in the hollow of the furrow—one day, joy; another, melancholy.

> ETAPLES,
> *28 June, 1917*

I had my first taste of battle last night, not a real whiff, but a transmuted, a narrative to fire the blood and awaken the young adventure love. A Highlander described to me, in that curiously familiar style of the born narrator, how he once led a water-carrying party to the front line. There was much racy detail, much quaint invention to give a variety, much I cannot remember, for it was tenuous in substance and as intimate a part of the tale-teller as his dusty kilt or war-worn balmoral. Night supplied the background; he had been detailed with six men and a guide to bring two tins of water. The party found the material all right, but on setting out discovered the guide had lost himself. Then they went on blindly, like Narcissus in the wood, going where fancy led, trusting to Providence and endowed with a fear of German 5·9's. Once the "Johnnies" took fright and sprinkled the sky with a constellation of star-shells, rockets, flaming comets; instantly they dropped down like stones or lumps of earth, and when the exhibition ceased, proceeded. At last they found themselves standing in a shallow trench that barely touched the knees. Realization came suddenly, that they were in the heart of No Man's Land, and down they went again. Then panic entered, confused their wits, and all took to their heels, leaving the precious water behind. The Captain was of opinion our friend had gone " west " with his party, for they were long overdue, and in the darkness might have walked into the welcoming arms of a " Johnny " ; naturally, he could scarcely believe his eyes when he saw the prodigals return, without a scratch and only one casualty, the loss of the water. When I heard that, I thought after all the sordid side does not remain the predominant : if I had such a tale to take home and narrate to an admiring audience, the danger would be worth while in this exaltation. " That man has been to hell and seen strange sights ", they would think with as much awe as the Florentines when they met Dante. If the battle-field only held such horrors as Dante has depicted, bravery would remain at discount, and the clean fearlessness of the soul arise in itself, like a purifying flame, burning agony to beauty and the loathsome to an eternal graciousness. I feel a kindliness in Dante's villains ; fatalism rests the religion of all, and the fatalist wills no evil to others : if the spectres rush at him with intent to kill, I can never divest myself of the idea that even at the end their threatening would change to indifference. A peculiar kindliness ! But in dreams there darkens no real horror, and no clutching grasp ever succeeds in uprooting the heart. So far, no farther ! the legend may say to the over-zealous. Even now, when in the depths of air I hear a dull thudding of guns, I am buried in my dream, like a chrysalis in the cocoon, and no outer disturbance will ever awake me : ecstatic moments come and melancholy till I can only hope for a consummation which in heart I desire not : dark hours come when every man rests unsympathetic and hostile, when self-content dies away and I long for a helping hand : but the dream substance remains, unchanged and unchangeable, the power to re-create a world and define a strange, new landscape of longing memory. He told me how he ran from the battle-field with a wounded arm until beyond the reach of fire, and then, sitting down, bandaged it. My over-intent imagination seized on it until he seemed a devil rushing up from a pit, like those in the Inferno, waiting to throw others into the depths.

Perhaps, in the future, when I have passed through it all and halted on the borderland of dream, I might recount every adventure and feeling into a great, undoubted epic, the rise and fall of a soul.

ETAPLES,
24 June, 1917

The human side flowers from the brutal, and if the war has done nothing else but spread a melancholy tale, it has written in words stronger than flame that the quiet affections remain greatest and most immortal, and have their own peaceful power to subdue the warrior-instinct. I think the latter is dead now: the old " Death and Glory " has become a sober introspective longing for the calm retreat into repose—rest, the one glory. The sickness of every man remains incurable, home-sickness with a most poignant looking-back and balancing of past delight.

Last night I ventured forth to see how the camp looked by moonlight. Then, I was sorry painting found no place in soldiering, and art must step back before behemoth. Spectral they stood, the long lines of tents with a wavering gleam stealing among them like a fairy brushing to silver with her wings. Grey-green earth and an infinity of pointing stars ! I thought peace had winged and found here a haven, all struggle gone to immobility.

From here I can see the blue of ocean quivering along dunes and shallow lines of forest purpling beneath an edge of chalk-hollows on green moors. Three little French boys are rolling over each other merrily, oblivious of anything savouring war. Three little, round-bellied goats, black and white, with big udders, are trying to seize a mouthful of shrub before the string draws them off with a jerk. At last, after scampering among the bushes, they all rush away, and my last view is a pair of much patched trousers dangling from a fence as their owner tumbles over. The goat has disappeared.

ETAPLES,
22 June, 1917

The time of cherry-blossom has passed and red fruits hang like rubies over walls. Pears are almost ripe, and apples swelling. Those slight things are just everything to us now ; we look closely at the world as if to huddle all its beauty to our heart and go, richly endowed with that grace, into the unknown.

I relish the idea of leaving this awful place: danger and any kind of horror is preferable to this. There is no life here, only existence. The base remains a resting-place for birds of passage who halt there on their way from home to the trenches. Confined to camp, a dreary wandering among tents under a blazing sun, wellnigh blinded by the glare and bored to death—that's existence. I cannot summon resolution enough to read the very few books to be got: just now, Algernon Blackwood's *The Wave* puts back an hour or two from the burdensome monotony.

Every morning the camp clears for the " Bull-ring ", a training-camp among the dunes set high above the road. I confess the first view stirred me and gave me a taste of the glory of a great army: but it wore away, and I don't care now what happens. The sand-hills are fully two hundred feet high, pale pink and dotted with ragged clumps of grass, just as if a maddened bull had vented his fury on them and torn huge gashes in the green. On those gashes, thousands of men silhouetted at drill or bayonet fighting; nearer the road, bombers throwing dummies at tin-plates stretched along wires, and weary warriors struggling over a miniature battle-field.

Zola's estimate of Northern France seems about right : I am romantic enough in thought if not in feeling, but the dreariness of poverty-stricken villages with children clad in rags of every pattern and selling goods at enormous prices, "estaminets" and cafés innumerable, "cabanes" painted white with green windows and yellow doors, hillocky roads and miniature gardens remarkable for nothing edible, led me to think the beauty of France a myth and her glory a fabrication.

Boulogne, however, viewed from the sea, shone pleasantly enough in a wilderness of grey wall, grey tower, grey roads, grey piers, reflected on a clear grey of rippling sea. A harmony of pearly colour, appealing to the quiet sense ! We lay before the harbour some time ; children, standing on piers mouldy with age and rotten with the biting sea, cried merrily in an uncouth dialect—some were sporting, naked, round piles, breaking occasionally green shadows with the gleam of lithe bodies and struggling limbs ; others, pale-faced and dark-eyed, hung from the rails and shouted greetings.

I could have made a great picture of the

whole scene. Sailing-vessels swung slowly out to sea, brown sails bellying to the rising breeze, and fishermen crying as they pushed forward the jib-boom. An occasional motor-launch darted from among the confused mass of spars and funnels; quaint little things they were, with room on deck for about two men to stand in comfort.

On landing we were assailed with women carrying baskets of oranges, generously offering them for twenty centimes each. Boys, some with petticoats and long frocks, baggy trousers or light breeches, blue-grey caps of every known or imagined shape, all very much the worse for wear, begged for souvenirs. Some of them were melancholy enough, too old for their age, I should say; very calm and very quick in repartee. A noticeable thing: much jest but no laughter, much wit-cracking but not a smile. The very youngest held out tiny hands, and I don't know how many of us grasped them with relief that so much innocence should still flower. It was like touching home again.

Then we set out on the historic march from Boulogne to Etaples. Trees darkened the road with full mass of foliage, every leaf opened to the summer's breath—tall poplars and elms. From afar one could trace a road merely by those long shadows lining both sides. In quiet corners nestled quiet gardens, cherries ripening over walls and pears stretching heads above the stone. The wheat shook heavily to completed growth, and in its heart flamed scarlet poppies. One field, I remember, gleamed a remarkably beautiful combination of red poppy, blue cornflower or wild flax (I don't know which), and white daisies, rich enough to adorn a queen's robe or star the wings of an angel. A garden of wild beauty like this would be worth a century's toil at tulips, dahlias, gardenias, azaleas, and the like, for the effect was as natural as a cloud-shadow on the hills.

I have become acquainted with the inevitable Maconochie, a gentleman who does not improve with intimacy. The climate is one of extremes, too much heat during the day, and too much cold at night. When rain comes, it does not drizzle down, but falls in sheets. Last night I was continually on the move inside the tent, avoiding drops that showed too great a tendency to creep between shirt and neck. The idea remains general that the war will finish in a short time: if it lasts another year, God knows what the most of us will think. I don't concentrate any dreaming on it : fatalism remains the only means of warding off depression.

ETAPLES,
25 June, 1917

I have the same feelings writing this letter as a schoolboy composing an essay. Every little idea, every little sentence, must be squeezed out, with the result that instead of being juicy and concentrated it gets all the drier under pressure. I shall try to waken myself up with a little description. There is a sadness in the air : below me a bugle blows a plaintive " Last Post " in a graveyard beyond the hospitals, some fine fellow gone, after suffering.

From the hill the red-roofed Paris-Plage lies taut along the sea : this morning the sun crept over it, touching an occasional spire to silver, and resting content with a single bar of light while the poplar-covered land lay in shadow—but on the sea the fishing-boats nestled like moths on closed wings, or butterflies touching a blue-flowered meadow ; not a movement, not a sign of life. With the incoming tide the brown sails were gliding up the river in endless procession, up and down, with tiny boats rippling at the stern. At night the cattle, gaunt and brown, came down from the shadow of the woods, wandering mistily over the sand and stood knee-deep in the water. A small fisher-girl, carrying a bag of mussels on her back, staggered up from among them and disappeared among the bushes. That is the beauty of this country, the beauty of association and memory. Such trees inspired the Barbizons, such a tide welling greyly over sand the Dutchmen of last century. The deep sea is always a pure sapphire and the trees are heavily massed in shadow.

SAVY,
8 July, 1917

I have had a very vivid experience of the real meaning of that phrase in the "communiqués": "Action was delayed owing to bad weather". There were thirty of us packed under a marquee on a floor of bare clayey ground. The country gave no sign of commotion: a present odour of fresh fruit floating among the trees and a heat-haze hanging sapphire before the poplars. Woods and orchards crowded into valleys, tall, silver poplars projecting like pillars into the dim sky. Colour wandered in graceful lines from the emerald fields before the feet, where poppies splashed carmine to the faint tenuous shade, neither purple or blue, of distant foliage. Our camp lay on the round of a hill: to the left a beautifully proportioned spire rose up among the trees, and to the right a field of various crops—wheat, barley, potatoes, rye, and mangel-wurzels—shimmered like silver in the suspended light.

Before bedtime I had a glorious vision of frail cloud piled up to a sunset of delicate colour; clouds dappled with purple and rose formed a great outstretched wing over a pale sea of gold barred with grey near the hills, where the red sun gleamed ghostlike —huge, immaterial, like a contour of dream veiling a face.

During the night I stole forth, curious and greatly daring, to see the darkness in the shadowy trees. Over the hill came a boom from infinite distance, and pale flickering sheets of light hovered in the opal half-light like wraiths tumbling and swaying in dance. The summer lightning, it was, heralding a storm.

Then we hooked up the flap, got into painful postures under greatcoats, heads resting on balmorals spread on packs between the shoulder-straps, and straightway went off to sleep.

I enjoyed two hours' misery, following with agonized interest the efforts of an incapable stomach to digest Army biscuits, " bully ", and cheese. Two men were talking in a corner. Dimly listening, my ear took drowsy note of a strange attempt at wit. One said, " Oh ! I have plenty of jack-knives ". To which the other replied : " Your knives are no good, only meant to cut up side-streets." Then the most appalling thunderstorm broke, lighted up the sky with vivid lightnings. Round the tents they played until the place resembled a scene of gala, a medley of Chinese lanterns, hovered in balls of fire until we could see each other's face, fell in flashing veils below the patch of hill visible beyond the door. The booming and crashing of thunder surpassed any gun-crescendos our artillery could have attempted. Then the pattering rain began to come right through. I was stirred to action by a twin series of drops which traced accurate rivers along my chest and feet.

Necessity made us shift from the sides to the centre, where we lay, an indiscriminate mass of heads and equipment, until a bleak morning declared its desolation. I was soaked through in the right side, having discovered a pool of water streaming on my waterproof-sheet. Boots were filled with water, and the bag of iron rations appeared a mass of mud and sodden biscuits, more a poultice than anything definite. The man beside me reminded me irresistibly of a water-rat, caked with mud and shivering with the cold. His sheet had almost disappeared in mud. The parade-square was impassable, with chalky clay which stuck like glue to the boot-soles and made progress a matter of earnest endeavour not of willing feet, an effort of will rather than a play of muscle. Running was absolutely out of the question.

ISEL-LE-HAMEAU,
9 July, 1917

The battalion has been out for a considerable time in a little old-world village twenty miles from the firing line. We entrained from the base in comfortless, windowless carriages to within eight kilometres from our present station, stayed at a depot camp overnight, and next afternoon marched on here, bending painfully beneath a full pack, 120 rounds of ammunition, a box-respirator, a P.H. gas-helmet, and iron rations. The shrapnel-helmet weighed like lead. The strain of the march became so great that runnels of sweat flowed down the face unnoticed until the hand, pushing back helmet, encountered moisture.

A continuous stream of motors passed, some camouflaged in a weird conglomeration of tints, the zebra-type of protective coloration. Mounted on the latter were guns of medium calibre, naval I should say, painted in line with the vehicle so that at a distance the whole appeared indeterminate.

Uphill all the road, with windmills decorating the landscape, sails motionless in obedience to the Sabbath dictate. We met parties of women and girls, " endimanchées ", coming from chapel, and a French priest, massive as one of Denny Sadler's creations, robed in " soutane ", and bareheaded, blessed us once when we lay resting by the road-side. Beneath a poplar, by a farm-house, drowsed two artillerymen, drunk as lords. Their fate, if an inquisitive Staff-officer concerned himself, can be imagined. At the hill-top, the country lay spread out in wonderful beauty of vanishing perspective until the grey sky completed its harmony. I could appreciate its quiet radiance and pure elegance of line, trees by long roads and blue shadows of hills at the horizon, for I had drawn such at home, attempting to realize its quiet infinity.

A tiny spire above a hedge of elms marked our village, and we came to rest with great thankfulness beside the town " mairie " on a muddy street.

> Isel-le-Hameau,
> *12 July, 1917*

At present, I try to blind one side of my imagination and direct the other to rustic felicity. You know the usual heroic cant, Phyllis and Amaryllis, plenty of shade and a profusion of trees. The " Open County " touched me for once : if the war is kind enough to overlook me, I can act Senhouse to the life. Last night I spent " à la belle étoile " under a sufficient service overcoat on a waterproof-sheet, washed in the mess-tin on the grass at morning, and generally aped an Arcadian illusion.

To-day one of Meredith's storms overcast the sky. The clouds rose, pier by pier, rugged tower by tower, until they grew top-heavy, lost shape in the mass, and resembled basalt cliffs glooming over a green sea. Houses and street appeared toy-like and puny beneath them ; figures, marionettes ; the soldiers, children's playthings, awaiting the disposal of a hand. Even now there is a rattle of musketry and a continuous patter on the tiles; the heavens blow great guns, and the forked lightning comes up from beneath like a flash on the footlights. The good wife emptied out her tank in readiness for a flood. The atmosphere was rather strong where the old stagnant water flowed from the pails. So far, however, her hopes have been disappointed, for the tank-bottom is still dry and the rain going off.

I shall try to obey your wish. The one and only original carries the sweet name of Thompson, no descendant of the poet. His vocation is rifle-grenadier: all his talk naturally centres round the absorbing theme of grenades. He threatens with them, as one would with a blow. One adjective summarizes all the descriptive material at his command, " bon ", pronounced very Scotch with a flavour peculiar to Thompson. This bed is " no bon " or " tress bon ". One gentleman confided to me the fact that his lordship wasn't quite right " upstairs " : as a matter of fact, I have had to gather my senses together sometimes to believe otherwise. No connection or apparent thought links in his talk, a rapping out of snappy phrases like bullets from a machine-gun, very effective, too, at times, as many an unfortunate humorist has discovered.

A master of farce without knowing it, witness his version of the old saw, " The older the fiddle, the better the tune ", as " The older the tune, the better the fiddle ". A helpless attempt at wit that sets laughter going instinctively. He is always wool-gathering, thinking perhaps of Bridgeton, late for meals.

Yesterday he came tramping in among the hay at midnight, in pitch-darkness, and settled down comfortably with one odorous foot on my face and the other in air, dangling over the edge. Of course, I protested, whereat he shifted his feet and put them on some other face. Shouts and curses came here and there till Thompson, very blasphemous, collapsed in a corner.

I think Shakespeare's advice applies with peculiar force to him : " Neither a borrower nor a lender be." Our friend obeys the first part with great scrupulousness, for he has never anything to lend. The second he disobeys with complete unconcern and a brazen effrontery that wins the day whether the victim wills it or not. He has been known to borrow half a stick of chewing-gum. I used to think few appetites could approach the average soldier's, but Thompson cares nothing for food, leaves his bread lying anywhere, always appears in a muddle about jam, cheese, etc., and oftener than not comes off second best.

One childish love rests by him still. Every night he spends forty centimes on a canteen full of foaming milk fresh from the cow, and the delighted way in which he laps it would serve as an inspiring study for Erskine Nicol or Webster.

I might finish with his appearance. In a sentence, he is an undersized, insignificant, dark-skinned gentleman, with dubious eye and brandy features, pendulous eyebrows and chin, never smiling or even laughing outright, but cackling like a consumptive hen. His tunic and trousers are piebald, black and khaki—black with grease-spots and tea-drops.

Isel-le-Hameau,
12 July, 1917

I can hear an insistent peal followed by a deeper bell-note in the grey morning, when the air grows chilly before sunrise. Surely the opposite of war, yet war's accompaniment, for the will releases its hold, and body and soul drink as at a fountain. A fine silhouette comes before the window, silver lines resting on the bent head and neck, flowing out to the elbow and descending legs until the sill cuts them short. An exercise of pure line, to be done by a pre-Raphaelite.

I can still find enthusiasm for my first idea that pure art lies in a fine line, that the great pictorial sublimity must have a definite foundation of perfectly wrought detail based to a great unity. There abides no reality in blurred masses of landscape or shapeless contours : the detail shows the artist as much as the ensemble. You remember how often I said that even a first-class writer could be defined by his descriptions of scenery.

Yet, gazing at the dunes and poplars of the Pas-de-Calais, the feeling arises that Corot was right, after all, in confusing earth and sky to a dominant vision. Taken minutely, leaf by leaf, a photographic reality reveals little power to awaken sympathy. The main value is atmosphere, and in its fold the masses of foliage sway in blue fringes, and veiled shadows vaguely foreshadowing a dream and hiding a greater presence.

The spirit of such a landscape may not be revealed in mere imitation, but in an exquisite harmony of clear opal colours—a pink ground of sand, faint sun-whitened cottages, a flock of sailing-boats resting with closed wings against the dim junction of green sea and green sky, a quiet river stealing to quieter cove, a girl driving cows along a grey road under a boundless heaven, a group of peasants talking round an open door, and a shimmering glory of white poplar and silver willow ruffled by the breeze. If I had only leisure and ability to realize the impressions this delicate landscape makes on me, I might in time become another Richard Furlong, bringing to nature its own speech and whispering its own message.

The swallows flicker and swoop from morning till night—on the highways, over the cornfields.

Often in this flat country, scenes beloved by Peter de Wint come into being quite unconsciously. The open appears a quiet combination of half-cut crops waving to an infinite azure and gold. Then suddenly perception coming from within declares it otherwise, and the women bending over the sheaves and covering them with their shadow remain statuesque, the eternal picture in an eternal cornfield, a creation of blue shadow in a sea of gold, golden air and golden land.

The shimmer inspires beauty, beauty of

quivering atmosphere splendid with fine detail, —red flowers just a speck on the ground, pink mallows lurking in retired corners, haughty yellow flowers rising above the wheat, and a generous display of heavy heads nodding drowsily against each other.

Then a flood of homesickness turns reflections bitter in the mouth. Only to live the present, when the future has no power to declare itself and be moulded by a soul's development, and the past seems useless to inspire a new conception—what a life ! Yet it must go on, day by day, until the hand declares its work and the finish comes, the decree that life shall continue, earth receive full development after a temporary interruption. That constitutes the darkness of war, gives the prison-house flavour, for no one knows what the morrow will bring forth, and what meaning yesterday may have in the unfolding of events. Even if the knowledge came that the end would be in a month, the heart might grow accustomed to the idea and prepare for the consummation. But everything rests in the lap of the gods and we simply lie, pinned down by an undeclared design, unable to move, unable to think clearly. A fine end to a youth of struggle, overcoming obstacles on its way to a broader culture, and we suffer it all for an idea of country that has no real existence in our thought.

AVESNES-LE-COMTE,
14 July, 1917

I often think when we walk here after a cup of coffee at the cross-roads, that few countries can lie so peaceful, so full of impressions which float in the air and meet no obstacle to their permeating influence, force the thought to quiet things—sunlight gliding past a window, touching the sill with white fire; nodding of leaves in the shadow; groups of old women beside the dung-heap, where the hens are bobbing; and long shadows of cloud on the flat plains.

It seems as if we had fallen back a generation and touched on the origin of things. Looking up into the roof of our billet, I can see the beginning of Gothic architecture, branches and beams mounting until their tracery becomes confused, and wonder is how they all keep together. The billet was once a barn; a rude door leads down into it from the yard, then we clamber up a ladder across a wooden platform down to a hollow on the other side. A shuttered opening gives light at day and cold at night, for the wind has a habit of stealing through the chinks and freezing the toes. The view enframed by it is very peaceful, a massive wave of ash-foliage, streaked and starred with sunlight, with a corner of red-tiled roof glinting above it. Two butterflies rise and fall across as they come from leaf to leaf, and occasionally a wet nose glides round from an inquisitive cow.

Isel-le-Hameau,
17 July, 1917

Of my comrades, Parkson is the most remarkable, not that we are a wonderful lot at all, but he has preserved a gift of rapid and suggestive description which the war brought into relief. As on a winter scene at Ypres : " You can't imagine how lovely the country looked at night : miles and miles of white snow with barbed-wire standing out in sharp silhouette, every barb visible and cruelly suggestive in the shadeless luminance. Just a clump of skeleton-like trees and a fold of mound ; on the sky-line great flares from the German trenches and Very lights glinting and falling till No Man's Land became clear as day and ghastly as a nightmare. The dead Germans lying prone on the ground appeared alive with a frightful flickering as if the passing through death had awakened them. Ruined buildings became set like definite creations chiselled from darkness, every contour clear and sharp, till one would have thought the builder had built them so in obedience to an overstrained imagination." With the addition of outspread arm and quick gesture, Parkson made the scene very vivid, dramatic at once.

If I can come through the mill as unshattered as he, I shall consider my experience of life complete, my apprenticeship finished. Optimistic, always expecting peace, scanning the papers for any little suggestion that may help him in his obsession, he has the ability to inspirit the poor new-comer who comes like one of Dante's unfortunates, body turned to his destination but head facing back to the home whence he has come. He quickly dispelled my gloom, and awakened that old delight in wit I thought had faded to oblivion and become lost in the pall. I have never been brighter in my life; I can remember everything with great clarity, assimilate picture and metaphor to a definite comparison, look back over my stock of poets and artists and compare their creation with what touches me.

Combined with this, the capability of

snapping off a pregnant remark flavours his conversation, imparts to it a rare essence, as " The privilege of being able to do a thing is not to do it ". I don't know whether this is old or not, but in his mouth it sounded the sincere result of thought, certainly not of platitude. He possesses the æsthetic sense in part, understands an obscure discussion, can moralize intellectually, and discuss literary subjects with a plenitude of natural force, even if he has not read so consumedly as I. The critical sense, as I would appreciate it, is there in embryo and would flower, I believe, given a definite culture.

The narrator of *Lord Jim* could touch the little things that culminate in a living impression, for Parkson has them in no small quantity ; but being no psychologist I can only voice the impression he makes on me. Perhaps when I know him longer, the present attraction will wear off and leave him a bald, dry figure, underneath a mask of word and phrase. But even the possession of the latter remains a rare thing, something desired by many, realized by few. After all, if sympathy consists in acting the listener to one who confesses, in absorbing the sincerities of a passion forcing way to utterance, the benefit is sufficiently great for one even if it may be a negative virtue without the power of assimilating and replying to confession.

Perhaps, when inspiration comes, I could see clearly into him and examine idiosyncrasies, but now the figure of the man stands before me and blinds perception like a landscape blotted by a silhouette. He has no illusions about war; says definitely his vocation never ran in parallel lines with war. There flowers no beauty from a war of sacrifice other than this, that, when the last cries shall have died down and the last great agonies come to rest, the eager spirit, warming to a rosy dawn, noble and enthusiastic with all its duties clear before it, will rise and create a new world as the Greeks dreamt it, when passion will be a quiet beauty and life a peaceful gliding to rest.

.   .   .   .   .

In complexion, Parkson is ruddy, freckled, and in feature, regular; in all a well-built type of man. That should be sufficient, for one cannot judge an intelligent being by a porcelain standard or submit him to a superficial criterion like a Dresden doll. Rather waken comparison by a prearranged conception, something wrought in the mind and framed in the intellect, tending more to a tenuity of image than to an insistence on handsome exterior.

Even as I see him now, with a pipe in his mouth, studying a paper while the daylight rests silver on the outline of face and stem of pipe, he appears a very ordinary person indeed, an end in himself, one of the least likely men to provide a subject for philosophy. But if Morley Roberts portrayed a grey type of man in *Henry Maitland*, surely I might concentrate imagination round a mere shadow perhaps, and evolve a definite figure. But what's the use of moralizing? Even if one could reproduce him in a living image, the old Narcissus taint would declare itself, and there would be a faint shadowing of self in another characterization, like Goethe breathing out his own image in Wilhelm Meister.

How far autobiography must enter into portrayal rests a matter for the great theorists who know how to practise in their own work what they outline in their criticism, to evolve a definite standard of comparison, something from the spirit to which the spirit can return.

I can see Gissing pouring out a confession in *New Grub Street*, defining for all that a living person, not a vague ghost of reminiscence. Reardon is as much Reardon as Gissing. Even if his message were confined to a description of a great struggle and submission of a great soul to circumstance (the submission death glorifies and brings to noble fruit, a portrayal of melancholy bordering on despair), the value of his narration would be one of great values, of unyielding standards. Only a universal type, a slight touch of a type known to all, whose agonies have been felt by every sensitive being, however dimly, a creature who had in his grasp the " blue flower " of genius, even to suggest that were the end of a mission, a fine finish to earth. The man who sets out to do that and succeeds cannot be counted a failure, but one of the chosen, whose knowledge can surpass a creation of stars and mount to the glorious end of attainment, the great empyrean of the fine soul.

When the mood comes for philosophy, out it comes willy-nilly ; anything can act as an excuse for utterance. But it seems rather pathetic to mix up questions of fine culture with the crude reality of war and its effect on the human. I can only reiterate in my mind the verse, " A cry of labour finding the sublime ", and comfort myself with the idea that the great beauties become only apparent after sacrifice, the gracious flowers of an earthly Elysium rise on a foundation of sorrow and grief, the only immortal creations find wing in a world of tear and fine altruism.

Isel-le-Hameau,
18 July, 1917

The discussion arose whether the real state can be a continuous join to earthly existence. Parkson was optimistic, as usual (I have never known him to take a sombre view of anything). I can only bless my luck for having a companion of such rosy views, this man " aux cheveux roux," as the old French dame calls him. It remains a mystery how the question arose. Perhaps the combination of deeply mottled evening sky gleaming full on us and the murmur in the yard of a young life—chickens crying round a mother—aroused an unseizable wonder that we should exist at all, and having lived, not exist again in a more finished form.

The five of us had elected to sleep out under a big walnut-tree, pendulous with green globules. At dusk preparations were made and sheets spread out. Flynn performed a waltz round us after he had gone for "doolay", and chanted a weird "mélange" of the most vapid revue-songs. The lady of the manor, an old relic, whose back and legs made an ideal obtuse angle like a bent bar without possibility of ever being straightened again, warned us, "Il fera mauvais temps", but comforted us with the assurance the tree would act as a fine umbrella. Very nice! After a little persuasion, however, she agreed to put a little straw in an outhouse which the hens had been using as a summer resort. We needed it before many hours elapsed.

I had been lying on my back admiring the clean-cut silhouette of leaves against the grey sky, and wondering how I could put them into a little cameo of description, when one huge drop closed one eye and a second fell into my mouth. We made a hurried exit—just in time, for the rain came down in sheets, quite unlike anything I have seen at home. There glinted and flashed a continuous lightning, and the wind droned through soppy leaves.

For that night we lay in the outhouse, and liked it so much that we have used it ever since. The Irish aspect appeals to me :

a narrow lean-to with tiled roof stretched on a sturdy framework of partly-dressed branches, with one wall of wood erected on a foundation of mouldy bricks, and another, opposite, of chalk-slabs, where one can trace memories of the war, as inscriptions :—

Delabine Paul,	or Bleu H. I. E.,
Classe 1900,	15 D'Artillerie,
15 Artillerie,	Année 1914,
Pas-de-Calais,	

and grotesque faces in a dim kind of relief. The third side has been blocked up with corrugated iron; the fourth looks on a quiet "mélange" of red-bricked chimney, pear-tree, and tall hedge—a yard where the hens congregate and peck all day.

I thought François Flameng painted his walls rather brilliantly, but when I look at the wall facing me across the yard, I can only wish he had used still more vivid coloration. The sun slants across and casts a warm reflection on the brick-face, flushing every shade, or even suggestion of shade, to a luminous half-light. There are greys, pale lemon, vermilion, emerald, carmine, faint amethyst, dark crimson, ochre, steel-blue, grey-green, white, and dark brown.

M. Ernest Delaby,
    Débitant de Boissons.

That seems the only type of shop-sign visible in a French village. The populace appears to live on " bière française " (a mixture of water and methylated spirit), " bière anglaise, vin rouge, vin blanc, grenadine ", a thick sugary substance made from raisins, " poires, pommes, prunes, framboises, groseilles, cerises "—everything, in fact, and used to sweeten other wines. Above a door may appear a white boot capped by the legend " Reparations ", but inside no boots can be seen, only a formidable array of glasses and bottles.

Flynn has a great aptitude for getting round the French. I think his Irish comedian face, with the spectacles, tickles in some way their sense of humour, and his grotesque attempts at French, " doolay ", " pang ", " no compris ", " mademoiselle " to everybody, even to the old " grand'mere " herself. Every night he goes round to the " patron " for milk and comes back with a foaming mess-tin full, " huit sous ". Last time I was curious enough to follow him and discovered him slipping a huge hunk of " pang " into his tunic, a present from the old lady.

I have been feeding on white cherries all the week; black currants, gooseberries, raspberries, and " salade ". It is rather amusing to be perched on the top of a tree and chatter French to the old gentleman hoeing in the garden beneath.

Avesnes-le-Comte,
18 July, 1917

Night and a slumber 'neath a shrouded tree,
Night and an arching white world overhead,
Then death dies and beauty comes again
   With melting smile and deeply shadowed eyes.

Night and an arabesque of jet,
The walnut's foliage cut against the sky,
Then thought wanders, life is but a sleep,
   A murmurous sinking in a deepening sea.

Night and one long sweep of branch 'gainst star,
And silent wings that shiver in the deep,
Then pain steals away, delight flies in
   And glory comes beside the welling tears.

Night and a thunder o'er the shadowy elms,
Appeal from out the bounds of earth and time,
A loved one's answer to my whispered hope,
   A voice that brings soul-longing peace again

Written in the afternoon at
VILLERS-SIR-SIMON,
22 July, 1917

Madame next door introduced her husband to us last night just after " lights out," a singularly intelligent type of the " laboureur ", a totally different man from Millet's conception. I cannot describe adequately how glad I was to encounter one who spoke pure French and had a certain amount of thought to his credit, one who had had enough clearness of conception to supply for himself the wisdom of books.

When face to face with fundamentals, the literary memory remains on the same level as the sensible, perhaps lower : together, if the mind can go clearly and straight, they arrive at the same conclusion and discover the same truths. It is a dangerous thing to disturb a philosopher, especially on the top of a beehive, and in many cases the French peasant was unconsciously a philosopher with ideas dormant until disturbance stung them into action.

We spoke far into the night, with the others lying in bed gazing curiously at us as we gesticulated and grimaced like animated marionettes in the flickering light of a candle.

The French armies, according to M. Geslairn,

consist principally of "laboureurs": the working class or industrial type, "mineurs, mécaniciens de fer ou de bois," etc., remain in civil life to a greater degree than in Britain. A father of five children does not go into the firing-line, but remains at the various bases. In all, no matter what category, they are absolutely sick of fighting, especially when a dim kind of socialistic unrest has begun to unseat hypocrisy. They cannot see what they are fighting for when their own men ravage the country as much as the Germans, and capitalists reap the wages of their endeavour.

The question of subsistence enters; for each child the soldier receives ·75 franc per week, for pay 5 francs per month, doled out fortnightly. The supply of officers is solved as carelessly as at home, any Tom, Dick, or Harry, literate or illiterate, may be recommended for a commission. Before the war the French aristocracy went into the Army as officers, all for the sake of a little glory won cheaply (" une petite gloriole "). They were covered with decorations (" tout galonnés "), now they differ from the private only through a little bar of silver, etc., on the arm. The aristocracy rests in the ranks : the idea of going first over the parapet and being exposed to the greatest danger doesn't appeal to them. Consequently commissions go to the foolhardy without regard to social position. Of course, the French armies have had an easy time this year : doubt is in us whether they mean to begin an offensive this summer or not. It is a matter of common complaint that our spring offensive, notably the battle of Arras, was ruined by the non-intervention of the French, who ought to have attacked at the same time as we. Of course, we know little about it : but it seems so disjointed, this way of limiting objectives and railing offensives to small areas. Let us all go over and finish the business in a mass.

My friend deplores the lack of education in France ; thinks Germany more educated. Only one in a thousand has enough culture to understand the reason for fighting and its abhorrent quality ; the rest, knowing no real master though obeying all, moulded by a dominant unscrupulousness, go into battle and die, perhaps, without having to experience the additional agony of imagination. The best fighters come from Brittany and round that region, because the Bretons are the most uneducated people in France. They have learned to battle for existence from infancy ; fighting has become an integral part of their nature—fighting with the sea, with a stubborn earth.

I remember having praised the French system of land division: but this interview darkened my ideas. No doubt the small land-holder exists in great number, but he can only earn enough to keep himself and dependants alive. The "Département" bears its own value; if it is populous, like the Pas-de-Calais, the "paysan" can find a fairly good market for his produce; in the Midi, where great towns are scarce, he has a hard time of it. His great curse is the "intermédiare". The latter arranges with the great carrying companies who transport the country's produce, and even if the peasant tries to sell his stuff direct, he finds his goods have been handed over to the middleman in transit. Consequently, till bound in a union, he remains helpless: in France the movement towards union is only in its infancy, lack of education being the deterrent factor. Prices become trebled in passage from the worker to the market, or rather the worker receives a third of the real value of his work. Impossible to remedy this, as the Government is really a union of "intermédiares". The discerning can see in this already a good motive for revolution.

Coming to agriculture, he told me of a method the southern French employ for reaping two crops of potatoes in the year. The potatoes are planted in Algeria, where the time for gathering appears to be March or April; from Algeria the seed-potatoes are taken in April and planted in France. That idea may be said to count in favour, for only " intermédiares " could do this. Cultivation in France rests purely intensive, except in preserves where big landowners shut off thousands of hectares for the purpose of holding great hunts, in the neighbourhood of Paris, for example. The hunting squire encumbers France as much as Britain.

Adulteration affects everything. Before the war, French beer was pretty good, remarkably pure; now the middleman has decreed that beer shall be bad, and bad it is, bad and dear. Champagne very often has no connection whatever with the grape, " le Vigneron " brand contains more honey than wine. Every French garden distinguishes itself by two products, " ruches " and apple-trees. The sour apples, not far removed from the crab, supply one of the ingredients of adulteration, honey the other. My friend told me of one characteristic of the German trader : the latter comes into France, buys up all the cider apples, makes champagne of them and exports the completed article to northern France.

I think I have dilated enough on land questions. I might come to the socialistic ideas of the man himself. He belongs to the thoroughbred type that made the French Revolution possible : sees not as in a glass darkly, but through a broad lens of humanity ; sees that liberty exists only in name, that there will always exist two types of man, the exploiter and the exploited. It is the peculiar business of the former to keep the latter blinded as long as possible, for he knows that when his slave becomes cognizant of real conditions his reign will end, and Barnfield's dirge can comfort him :—

> King Pandion he is dead,
> All thy friends are lapped in lead.

" Le peuple reste esclave enchaîné, même si l'on ne peut pas en voir les chaînes." He rolled that phrase over his tongue with a kind of Epicurean delight. The pessimistic strain colours his outlook ; perhaps when suffering will have changed his life too, and robbed it of its fruits, the noble thought might come of a great city of friends, where no man is greater than another save through fine character and beauty of life. He has gone thus far; considers the republic no more a republic than Germany. The only real republic will be a great union of all workers ("un syndicat uni"), where equal division will rule and man be valued by his work, intellectual or manual, and by that alone. Even the lilies in the field will show forth their beauty as a prize, the symbol of a gracious loveliness throned above human endeavour, the goal where eyes will turn at last and, satisfied, close in the peace of a great consummation, a task granted by God, and carried out in God's own way.

ISEL-LE-HAMEAU,
23 July, 1917

I am reminded irresistibly of George Morland when I look round the billets where our platoon is lodged, of that calm beauty of ancient rafter and lordly tree which bases a poignant appeal to the memory of a past delight. Bohemia come at last to the Bohemian in dream, who loves to dwell in shadows of his own imagination and strives to change a world to a dominant wish. I thought Morland's world something unreal, and yet here it is completely realized. Red tiles darkened by age to a warmer brown, buff walls of mud and straw stretched on branches like unreal shadows on a bas-relief, a profusion of climbing plants beyond flower and ripening to seed—wistaria, clematis, and an occasional wreath of ivy; quaint effects of cool colour painted on windows and doors, blue and pale-red; tiny panes peeping behind flower-pots, and a fine odour of fresh fruit—that is my village. Every house is owned by a peasant whose ancestors have had their peculiar idea of architecture, building sheds and house round the dung-heap so that the good wife can spend a happy day gazing on her hens.

Beyond stretches the allotment with a single heavily laden cherry-tree, two magnificent walnuts with green fruit hanging at the branches' end, sweetly and powerfully scented with resin, a row of white poplars, and two green meadows bending over the hill. Tethered in one of them, a large brown cow, having grazed its circle of country to the last shoot, chews the cud, while a smaller edition wanders at will among the trees.

II

THE SOMME

LIGNY-ST. FLOCHEL,
25 July, 1917

I WONDER when I shall escape the art obsession. Not that I want to escape, for the only relief from melancholy lies in a generous giving of imagination, a wholehearted surrender to delight to a need for image. To-day the Barbizons occurred to me again when we journeyed from billets to a Trench Mortar School. The country, to the shimmering wave of horizon, stretched back in a delicate intertexture of line, flat as a board and only darkened by an occasional cloud-shadow or a sun-shadowed clump of tall trees hiding a village or château. Nothing in it resembled my own country, and insensibly I began to have a faint understanding why the French landscapists emphasized and found so much inspiration in the figures of peasants at work in the fields.

In such a quiet harmony of fields the

moving figure, whether animal or human, remains the centre of interest, and not being far below the skyline always possesses the additional charm of silhouette. In the lapse of projecting land-peculiarity, the French peasant appears unconsciously a symbol, a method of natural utterance. The eye fixes on that one object and understands the surroundings by comparison : woods and meadows, instead of supplying the interest, only serve to enhance the importance of the subject. Either the woods are treated " en masse " and form purely woodland landscapes, or they are viewed in purple perspective, shadows against the horizon. I have never seen in French art those wonderful natural combinations of mountain, valley, and river our Scottish artists delight to render on canvas ; only a flat atmospheric decoration round a symbolized figure or a great scene of lofty tree, sun-streaked or bathed in mist at dawn or evening.

.   .   .   .   .

Last night our company waited for three hours beneath an avenue of lofty trees, from falling dusk to darkest night. We had come from the Brigade sports in full expectation of meeting transports which would take us

THE SOMME

to a village fifteen kilometres away. But, in accordance with rule, none arrived. So we lay down and tried to sleep on our equipment, using box-respirators as pillows, in the forlorn hope of going away every moment. As time went on, some strayed away and few returned, with the result that half the company was drunk with " vin rouge." At last, Johnson and I, chilled to the bone, slipped away on an exploring expedition, and discovered wire-netting beds at the village cross. We hadn't been there three minutes when fall-in sounded, and away we all marched, a disorderly rout, murmurous as " flies on summer eves ", singing simultaneously every song the music-halls have created for man's misery. Jolted along rutty roads we retraced our steps until we passed the windmill before the village, and dropped exhausted into our old billets at two o'clock in a grey morning.

All along the skyline, beyond the dim shadows of trees, summer lightning was flickering and flashing like the flare of big guns. Not a light was visible anywhere, only the misty twinkle of stars from an infinite sky. We appeared invisible along the sunken road beneath the shadowy pillars of trees, like spectres wandering from one bourne of mystery to another, creations of night marching to dawn. I think the sole beauty of war lies in the contrast—clash of arm and peace of dream.

Even when we lay under the trees there was a mystery in all that approached the unreal. Occasionally a sparkle from a match sent light shooting up the trunks among the leaves, and cast a weird chiaroscuro on men grouped on the road or stretched out, bringing harsh features into ghastly relief, and darkening hollows until they were like deep pits. Eyes were lost in darkness, and only one side of the nose gleamed whitely: khaki changed to hodden-gray in light, and in shadow disappeared altogether. A strange beauty rested on all and veiled memory with its own peace. Little groups whispering beside the road and under the hedges, isolated pairs walking up and down almost unseen, a faint contour of figure stretched along a doorway or beside a wall—all seemed lost in a universal harmony, the last harmony that reconciles the earthly with the unearthly, the warring with the peaceful, the rebellious with the acquiescent, until an immaculate consummation shall touch all to one and unite all in a final conception. I think the noblest could have found in such a picture a great frame for suggestion, and known a realization of the juncture of spirit and body as the only perfection.

Even as I write, in a peaceful orchard, under a darkening sky, where a rose-gold sunset has died away behind a fine symmetry of twisted trunk and branch and shadow-laden foliage, red-tiled farm buildings rising above a hill, when an aeroplane emerges from the faint purple cloud-light and drones away to the distance, I cannot believe war is real, or anything else, but a dream, entirely divorced from reality and outside of human thought. The spirit flies away to an indefinite joy in longing, and the eye sees but inwardly, reconciling silent tree, pigeons on the roof-top, green grass and twisted branch to a faint desire, a dim pain distantly poignant, and the vision, resting from anguish, dreams of its own world and finds peace in vision.

Isel-le-Hameau,
28 July, 1917

I have a peculiarly distinct memory of a wonderful dream-picture seen last night. I had been sleeping fitfully without opening my eyes, half-conscient of things and sensitive to tenuous imaginings, when a resolution came to wander out under the trees and look at the giant in the grey starlight. This giant was a strangely fashioned shadow of foliage against the sky, tall trees overlapping so that he appeared to be rising from sleep, head and shoulders above the coverlets.

The sudden image called forth a curious echo, involuntary as a cry when one falls into water, a swift shrinking and a sharp pain suddenly gone, a faint fear that penetrated to the utmost depth of unseizable perception and touched chords unsuspected before.

That was the first time, and then I thought the shadowy attitude implied menace, but, as I see it every night since, the indistinct grows luminous and the darkness is full of the gleaming of eyes—kindly eyes looking down on me, like a Sphinx become benevolent. Sometime imagination might evoke a smile, a smile of good portent. I can see a child grown wise under that shadow and flowered to a dreamy youth prior to clean manhood, grown to a quiet perfection of imagination and reality—colouring thought and soul which should bring him to a mystic wonder, an education of natural beauty as unsuspected as the dew from evening skies. Another

Joan of Arc might find a second great mission visualized. If I were to remain here a long time, I believe its presence would become as real to me as the men sitting smoking before me with the reflection from sunlight imaging a sharp contour of feature.

I wakened up and thought the moon was shining outside. A pale diaper of silver lay traced on the wall, cutting across a fragment of beam and chalk-slab. Outside, however, only the stars shone, clearly and strongly, with a firm though subdued light. Nothing definite showed but the great giant-shadow on the edge of woodland: here and there a tree-trunk gleamed dully like pewter, contourless, and lost farther up in the broad darkness of foliage. The grass shone grey with an occasional flicker of dewdrops. The harmony lay in diaphanous gradation of beautiful pale colour, rising to misty light and falling to pearly shadow.

The beauty was enshrined in perfect stillness, so perfect that the spirit felt at one with surroundings, and there remained no obstacle to a junction of earth and mind, all one beat in a fine consummation. One would have thought the trees were pillars in an old Italian garden with naked gods and goddesses gleaming whitely, Pan and his satellites living once more and moving mysteriously in the shadow.

.   .   .   .   .

You know that passage in Timothy, and may get from it my justification for casting thought of war aside and looking farther: " No man that warreth entangleth himself with the affairs of this life; that he may please Him who hath chosen him to be a soldier ". The question only remains, who chose me, was it God or Government? Free-will didn't send me; perhaps Providence selected me. Would it be a good thing to please the one if the latter, or good to please the other if the former? Does He grant subsistence and reward for the sufferer even when the sufferer does not see the justice of his cause and rebels in his heart against war?

That brings me to one who symbolizes and resumes in himself the contrasting elements I have brought into relief. This man is one of the fine spirits I have known, not a polished but a rude form, cut in the Michelangelo type, " cornerful and dark ", too old for fighting and old enough to put a fragmentary originality into his thought. He acts orderly-corporal for our platoon and distributes letters, rations, papers, etc.; has been in the firing-line during the spring advances and experienced their horror.

He told me of a horrible experience he had in the trenches. After a costly advance on the Thursday of 23 May (I think), near Fampoux, I expect a kind of brain-fever had seized on him, a final overflow of bile from the dreadful sights he had encountered, mere fragments of men, limbs, heads, bodies, sundered and dead, lying in heaps, especially in a quarry near the village—a whole communication trench choked with his own comrades killed by shrapnel. Anyhow, whenever he looked at a soldier beside him, the latter appeared an enormous giant, distorted and horrible. The trench held a long succession of such Goliaths let loose to destroy humanity. Everywhere he turned the same enormous faces glared at him until, frightened to the last soul-depth, he cowered in a funkhole and tried to beat down the obsession. But the odour told him he was lying on a corpse, a German uncovered by the digging, and away he went, bowed beneath his mental burden, broken for that time and broken for ever.

Speak to him of trenches and he will burst out into bitter expressions of despair, as one with whom nightmare has been a living thing and a constant bedfellow. By a weird irony the trench where he had such a frightful experience was called " Cupid " trench, as if love could enter such a cesspool or common humanity survive such a blow. It is horrible to think that clean life should have such a consummation, and immortality recompense such agony.

That is the great impression one gets of the man, that he has passed through a time of horror. It gleams in his eyes, in his nervous manner of speech, in the queer fits of pawky cynicism which come over him and inspire sharp utterance of uncomfortable truths about life. I cannot remember any of his phrases now, but some of them possess an original value and depth like those in *Feverel*: he has been in the pit, breathed an atmosphere of decaying mortality until even the quiet delight of a holiday under the trees has not complete power to vanish memory or bitter recollection. A soul arrested in its passage through darkness to light, dimly aware of past happiness and suffering still from the haunting miseries of death seen face to face even as the reaper was laying his swathes.

I used to speak of Schiller's inability to

THE SOMME

unite poetic temperament with reality and produce harmony, thinking that only in a poet could this state occur, but in this man who did not trouble with flowery thought of speech, whose last idea would have been an explosion into poetry, the same struggle has arisen and will never be solved. In quiet civilian life he won't be able to forget, and even when war is over and become a thing the mind willingly forgets and shrinks to remember, when everything of life will be concentrated on the arts of peace, he will remain a twofold being, not entirely at rest nor entirely reminiscent of war—something of both, not all of one.

That is the tragedy appealing always to imagination: generous, magnanimous when necessity arises for its practise, careful of life as of its detail, clean in conduct, he will be for me the type of man whose finest qualities have been emphasized by war, stamped in pure relief by the solid imprint of a horrible experience. Creedless, perhaps, before war, he has a creed now, something deeper and better than a belief in Christ or the phenomena of spirit and Godhead; something unseizable and evasive that goes to the heart and enunciates a fine philosophy of humanity and a love of clean life spent in peace and developed in liberty. A cynic without knowing it, not the modern type, but that fine old Greek, who believed in sacrifice as a means of obtaining grace ; who preached good for its own sake, and altruism as its own reward. As he said in a more intimate moment, " The thought has passed through, and the spirit, bounded by a sweet beauty of dawn, will go on towards a broader and clearer existence. That is the aim and end of philosophy—my philosophy—and that will be surely enough to commend me to destiny. No Christianity or a ranting of hymns, but a trust in the boundless and inevitable. That is all and enough for me ".

BERTINCOURT,
5 August, 1917

We came down here from Arras along a famous road, or rather a road that will be famous in our future history. From Arras to the Somme, a transition from a peacefully complete landscape of full-foliaged trees and flowering fields to a recent scene of desolation, where Nature is only beginning to cover up her wounds with a profusion of verdure and scented grasses ; where the trees lie in mere fragments and the avenue roads have lost their poplars and elms, rising to a bare skyline and immense overhanging sky. At dusk our buses passed through Bapaume, and with a dying sun falling in a blaze of gold from the sky, came on a straight road rising and falling in regular succession for miles. Dusk came suddenly, and darkness so clear against the horizon that a near hill seemed to lead to a great sea of mystery, immaterial as a dream. Behind us the road was a winding snake of many jewels, buses succeeding one another at regular intervals; occasionally we passed an obscurely lighted " château " or " estaminet," the walls and façades vaguely splendid in the uncertain light. I don't know how long we travelled thus, but it stirred all the most romantic imaginings, this journey across a desert country, once inhabited and cultivated, now a wilderness starred with holes or crowned with lonely groups of white crosses, strewn with ruins of houses. Bapaume was a gaping wreck, not a house but lay open to the winds; yet in the orchard were pears and apples; flowers hung over the deserted and desecrated gardens. In a grey dawning we came, spent and weary, to this village abandoned by the Germans in March and given to the flames. But memory will cleave to that vision of serpent-like road coming through a grey monotone of desert country—memory of beauty seen in a finer rebirth.

BERTINCOURT,
3 August, 1917

Romance flavours life more and more : the fantastic appearance of a high grass seen over a trench parapet at night, when Vèry lights transform the nodding clumps of wild flax and charlock into trees ; the sliding and crunching of a company on a night-march over marshy country, when the sunken road gleams grey-white like a canal and the mud rises knee-deep ; now the wandering of memory among piles of official papers scattered promiscuously over wooden beams, shattered columns, carved capitals, incomplete pediments, and mouldy bricks.

Especially to me, the past has always been a living thing, ennobled in the finer things— literary movements of a century linked with political, living authors in the dead whose voice is never silent but speaks to the memory. You can understand how that feeling is, of familiarity in a life and culture long past, when a name calls up all that that period meant in its own estimation and what value it has in ours, dead hands beckoning and an appeal that is never still.

THE SOMME 65

I picked up *Le Bulletin de la Société Protectrice des Animaux* (1873) and saw the name of Alexandre Dumas, Jun., as one of the collaborators. Instantly the whole period came up before me, that time of spiritual malaise after the founding of the Republic, when literature became over-sensual in one direction and over-melancholic in the other; when love declined to the lustful, and no fine hope of development raised literature above great art into great creation; when Maupassant, Flaubert, Dumas, George Sand, exalted passion over truth and subdued life to mere existence swayed by violent feeling. The contrast of that time and its recollection with the ruins around me seemed, strange enough, a touch of irony.

Then a sheet of manuscript written in a childish hand :—

Composition du 28 fevrier, 1860 (Corbier Jean-Baptiste).

C'est le Seigneur qui opère les merveilles dont nous sommes témoins. Dieu est le souverain de nos âmes.

Composition du 5 fevrier, 1869.

Les sciences ont des racines amères, mais les fruits en sont doux. Pardonnez à tout le monde et même à vos ennemis.

There is a pathos in that, in that silent writing, as if a face had come between,

F

hauntingly, with a dim shadow of smile, and a hand had touched, appealing. So many lives, perhaps as simple as this one, with no monument other than this, no other memorial but a faded copy of old morals written many times with a halt and strain to intelligence to comprehend to the full; many errors of spelling, but never an error of thought. How true they sound even now, the old tags! " Pardon every one, even your enemies." It seems a fine answer to our striving, especially when the home has been reduced to ruin and a mass of bricks covers the only traces of memory. They were sufficient for them, surely they can be for us.

Composition du 27 juin, 1863.

Le printemps commence ; la végétation se ranime. Les feuilles des arbres poussent. Les prés verdissent. Les oiseaux chantent dans le bocage. Dieu a fait de rien le ciel, la terre, la lune, les étoiles, les anges, les pommes, les animaux.

Evidently the good village padre was the schoolmaster : there is a good smack of homely religion behind those exercises. A quiet commune with little of external interest, everything intent on narrow circles of work and neighbourly intercourse, visits from " le bon curé " and to the chapel. It seems the acme of tragedy, this quiet appeal from hearts which perhaps do not beat now, and whose only purpose lay in a peaceful devotion to labour and a final gliding to rest.

A whole crisis in history is visualized in the names of two papers :—

Journal Officiel de l'Empire Française, vendredi, 26 fevrier, 1853,
Journal Officiel de la République Française (1873) ; or
Le Moniteur Universel de l'Empire Française (1854),
Le Moniteur Universal de la République Française (1879).

The swift transition from an empire to a republic, wrought by a time of unequalled disaster and negatived by time until the new republic differs but little from the old empire. In 1871 the ideal would be dominant, and the ideal would come to victory only in the heart of those who actually fought for it : with time the lapse into the usual coincided with the disappearance of the old generation, and now the only mourners for the lost ideals are historians seeking a text for preaching liberty, or moralists trying to sympathize in heart with what they stood for, seeing in name a memorial to the futile, a tragedy of baffled endeavour. France has never changed very much since Napoleon ;

judging from *Le Journal des Communes*, the principle remains practically the same.

A new perspective of war arises when one sees a village left by the enemy, everything completely wrecked, even fruit trees cut down to the ground. It appears so senseless, destroying harmless apple- and pear-trees; but the flowers survive and grow over the ruins. The simple beauty becomes more wonderful in contrast, and the great object in life grows not to a perpetual endeavour to overtop conditions, but to harmonize in them; to view Nature as a final and go with her, sure that the secret of her origin is ours, and ours in no way different; that there rings one voice in existence, taking up and echoing every one.

I have a feeling almost of hatred when I think at all of the ruined houses in this village. The pathos is not in broken wall or gaping room, but in the fact that a definite source and centre of human happiness has been cut off, their possessors thrown aside, helpless and out of place. So many lives, quietly lived, blown to the winds. Surely nothing can atone for that, no mouthing of principle or ideal destroy that impression. A seated melancholy, hands crossed in resignation until a new merriment will lighten up eyes and a new song ring in the silence. Until then, desolation and a memory of the past! That's all existence.

BERTINCOURT,
6 August, 1917

I'm enjoying life to the full here. Of course, I go out determined to be interested, and that makes all the difference. As La Rochefoucauld says in a scrap of paper I found beside the pond where the transport mules are washed :—

La douceur de l'esprit est un air facile et accommodant et qui plaît toujours quand il n'est pas fade.

While memory is still fresh, I might continue my description of labour among the rubbish heaps. In the whole village there were only three houses where literature made itself evident : one, a notary's office sprinkled with law-books and journals dating from the eighteenth century, and an occasional note-book showing that some one there had been attending a Lycée (I have one by me discussing French literature of the classical age) ; the second, the town office already described, with this addition, that records had been kept of the best scholars in the local school, judging from the "cahiers" lying scattered among municipal papers; a third, something like home, where an inherent taste for good literature had reigned without partaking of a purely academic character—a collection of books gathered from love of books, not from business motives.

You can judge of the delight I had in meeting old friends whom I had consigned to the past and only dreamt of meeting again in an improbable future. Although mouldy, tattered, green with damp, coverless, incomplete, they shone clear as life to me, like a battered Cupid in a garden. Even if the features were broken, the dear faces yet lived and found beauty in imagination. They stood for a past delight, and that delight threw a glamour over them and stayed by them in decay. I spent an afternoon thus, a strange Midas looking for gold, ecstatic when a treasure came forth or an especially valuable jewel gleamed to the hand.

Strange encounters! Fenimore Cooper's *Pioneers* in a French garb, and Dickens's *Cricket on the Hearth*, both thoroughly domesticated, judging from dog-ears and thumbmarks. Some of the great names in French literature lay there, glorious even in ruin: Hector Malot's *Romain Kalbris*; Rosny's *Valdemer*; Bazin's *Madame Corentine* (a well-preserved lady); Sand's *Histoire de ma vie* and *La Petite Fadette*, both sadly tattered and torn; Thier's *Littérature Française*, recognizable only in two complete pages; Gaston Boissier's *Madame de Sévigné*; E. About's *Alsace*, with its justification in the ruins round about it.

There were others equally valuable, but I can't remember, and I have no desire to go through the relics again. The sanctity of death hangs by them, and once disturbed, even if done in all reverence and appreciation, they retain no longer their beauty of ruin. Let the first impression stay, untouched by custom or repetition. When I found them first, they appeared to me like souls lost and needing a hiding-place, uprooted from their sanctum and at the mercy of the winds. It would be a strange thing to find, not a lovely flower growing from some dead Cæsar's head, but a tall grass, pendulous, with graceful awns, nodding and bending above a beautiful page from Sand or France.

Something like tragic irony that the authors who found nourishment and inspiration in nature should themselves give root to nature! Perhaps on a page descriptive of natural beauty a fine flower might grow, excelling the picture beneath. Both grades of life, the living grace and the living speech centring on one attribute, one beauty. Fromentin's *Une Été dans le Sahara* recalled that reflection more than any other book, for its great beauty lies in description, and description alone. I found it reclining beside a red poppy. Daudet's *Froment jeune et Risler aîné* lay in a corner beneath a muddy tile, poor Sidonie's loveliness a trifle tarnished by green mould and verdigris.

I could go on moralizing *ad infinitum*, but this must be a dry subject to any one but myself. The old joker dwells on his own jokes, forgetful of the fact that they have lost all point.

.   .   .   .   .

It is wondeful how the men of my platoon converted a tumbledown shanty of a peculiarly fine Hibernian type, roofless in part, choked up with bricks, floorless and windowless, with a solitary white jalousie dangling drearily from one hinge against a bulging wall, into a comfortable billet. At night we sit down before a blazing fire, made of beams taken from the house, and tell each other stories of the spring battles—Arras, Messines, Vimy, Fampoux, and Gavrelle. One incident at Fampoux sounded horrible enough, of an old quarry filled with dead Highlanders, and another how we left Vimy Ridge, breathless and spent with the speed of march, to get out of shell range. An amusing "contretemps" occupied my attention yesterday: a French doctor wished a fatigue party to dig beneath the ruins of his house for some buried valuables and requested the aid of our official interpreter; this interpreter could only speak French, and an interesting group was formed round the working-party, the town mayor, who only spoke English, and the two Frenchmen, all gesticulating together without making themselves understood.

There are some contrasts war produces which art would esteem hackneyed or inherently false. Of course, they have the power of life, and even a frightful travesty endowed with it might transcend the most ambitious effort of imagination. In a corner of the roof a swallow had built its nest before we entered into possession. At that time there were no doors nor windows to prevent ingress and egress, so that it was quite natural for the mother to choose this site. It had the main charm of being sheltered from the weather. Now, as the result of our efforts, only a small square hole lay open. Yet, from early in the morning until dark, the mother whizzed through to the corner, hovered at the entrance for a second, and then darted across to the nest. Quite a beautiful incident! Then the young ones left and sprawled along a narrow cornice, each to receive his share. All the while a great confusion of chirruping and cheeping. Her labour finished, the mother disappeared with a graceful swoop into the open. The delightful thing about it all was the trust placed by the birds in our kindliness, and we never disappointed them. The picture rung of home, had a tang of the domestic that rendered it sacred, as sacred as a porcelain Madonna in a way-side shrine.

Royaulcourt,
9 August, 1917

I might tell you of a night-march I went through last week. We had been in the trenches and were due to be relieved at nightfall. I remember the stormy sunset flashing and dying across the valley : purple clouds broken by shell-bursts on the hill-crest and a curling wave of white thinning down into air. The trenches lay deep in mud until we crept up on the parapet and walked along, knee-deep in wild flax, vetch, **ragwort**, and other heavy-headed weeds. The raindrops fell in showers from the plants over puttees and boots. A figure stationed here and there whispered directions or stopped us until the others came. The romantic aspect appealed to me at once: strange to say, the enemy did not stir at all except to send up a few lights, while our own batteries kept a continuous booming. One gun especially delighted me; it had such a clear hard way of spitting forth its projectiles.

Along hedges, by skeletons of houses eerie in a vague starlight, down a rutty street we crept, and then rested in a sunken road while the company gathered together. Whenever the leading files encountered an obstacle in the path, they sent back warning as " Shell-hole to the right ", " Wire ", " Plank ", or " Keep to the left ". With mud ankle-deep and tacky as glue, the warning was necessary. The ironic spirit must have chuckled when he saw our disorderly yet orderly progress across a bleak, wet expanse of grass, every one staggering from clump to clump, slipping into old boot-hollows, splashing puddles, and tearing through top-heavy bushes like ghosts after a midnight revel.

Decoration did not interfere with solid reality: the whole picture centred on a muddy group battling in shadowy greys and green obscurities, without chiaroscuro, bathed in an enveloping nocturne. Yet it was wholly satisfying: an occasional rise and dip of ground floating with shadowy mist, a bunch of trees formless and only a splotch of green-grey, white lanes by a forest and a dark mass of tree-trunk passed in silence—those were the only characteristics of the country. Not a sound penetrated the stillness other than the muffled roar of a gun or the faint whizz of a passing shell. Lanes of reddish light hovered across the sky—flame from a gun-muzzle. We spoke seldom and not loudly, passing a Very pistol at times, each man taking his share of the burden.

Sometimes we came from the clover-fields to a sunken road, slithered down into the mud, and scrambled up the other side, and so went on. The first road we met was so white with liquid mud that, looking up at it, I thought of a canal, and expected a wooden bridge. On discovering that no bridge was forthcoming, we went into it cheerfully. The Army so inures one that, even if the mud had risen neck-high, one would have struggled on.

You can have no idea how tired I felt: first

I shifted the rifle to the left shoulder and lessened the weight on the right by holding up the ammunition pouch, then vice versa the whole night through. The nerves were wearing to a very fine edge : irritability took the place of resignation, and slow anger at nothing at all the place of irritability. It is a fatigue like nothing else on earth. Not an excess of striving or strain of muscle—the physical enters little into it—but monotony grown poignant in toil, insistent dwelling of vision on a path which mounts to the brain and causes dumb agony. The spirit takes note of nothing, perception dies, and, like Christian, we carry our own burden, thinking only of it. Even if a will-o'-the-wisp floated hauntingly before and trailed seductive veils across the eyes, we would go on, with erect heads and straight shoulders, the dawn-like ardour in the eyes. The weight is little, the thinking much : yet, the journey ended, how little real fatigue remains!—how slight the pain to memory! There is a negative delight in recollection, and a gleam covers the obscurest and gloomiest trials of body and will.

We travelled then by light railway from Metz Wood to the ruined village I have mentioned previously.

.   .   .   .   .

A curious thing I have noticed in my travels is that, amid all the desolation and squalor of ruin, the crucifix remains untouched. Every cemetery is crowned by a Christ hanging from a high cross, gazing His eternal pain and message above those who have died with that vision in their hearts, flowers and tall grasses clustering to His feet. I have never seen one mutilated : even here, where shell-holes in tombs have exposed bodies, the figure remains immobile, immutable. There dwells a strange beauty, something that speaks quietly and wanders to the innermost, recalls a vague joy and touches a vague sorrow so far down in the spirit that we can scarcely perceive and are only dimly certain of its existence. The wild entanglement of shrubs and garden flowers—clematis, ivy, nettles, carnations, hyacinths, dead-nettles, hemp-flowers, marigolds, and poppies—appears just right : they say that nature and the human are one, devoted to a great religion symbolized in that lonely figure. I may not believe in Christ especially, but there dwells an abiding glory in that symbolism, a breath from the immortal to the immortal, something that lives in the perception of the unseizable beauty and floats higher than vision.

.   .   .   .   .

Real life is counted in affections, and perhaps if we were to analyse our profoundest feelings and throw all aside, there would remain at the last a memory of trust in a great example. Even when I see ruins lying around me of French hamlets, villages, and even country towns, I never can summon enough superficial sentiment to be angry at their desolation. The great healer will heal their wounds more quickly than ours.

Above me white balls of smoke float in the air, shells bursting round an aeroplane. And at the skyline a rounded shoulder appears, a cloud rising or falling back to dream on a bed of snow. All so peaceful, as incomparably homelike! Many a time I have seen Tinto spread out like a turquoise pedestal for those faintly flushed sky marbles. That was the beauty of home to me. I would give up everything to see them again, live like a beggar, abandon all hopes of success for a summer's afternoon in the hills, listening to the cry of curlews and the bleating of sheep. There is one great comfort : a definite good will come of our exile ; a new religion of life rise from our endeavour. The memory of this time may be in after years a treasured thing, when we fought a

Crusade for an ideal and manhood, proven, emerged clean.

ROYAULCOURT,
15 August, 1917

I am writing this from a dug-out made by cutting a square recess in a sloping bank and covering it with corrugated iron and earth. A rabbit existence, sleep all day, and a modicum of work at night. Entrance is gained by crawling on all fours through a low opening, slithering painfully over legs and bodies to a fixed place. War appears to be a matter of listening to a few whistling shells exchanged at long intervals, of marking out minute figures on a dull-brown hill-side crowned with trees and a phantom-like hedge of poplars. Not a movement anywhere; even the sun lingers more drowsily here than elsewhere, and the grass bends but seldom to uncertain winds. The old conception of a violent strife of combatants or even the modern of an inferno of bursting shells dies down to quiescence, and there dwells a sober touch about the whole landscape, as if it were alone given to droning bees, fluttering butterflies, and flitting swallows.

Last night the desolation received a quiet haunting beauty, the moon dreaming through

THE SOMME

haze from a dewy earth, mist lying in long swaths in every hollow and below the trees. There dwelt no foundation in anything, a barred nocturne of pearl-grey with dark shadows of foliage floating uncertainly like weed on water. The Very lights gleamed but faintly, and shells fell only after hours, as if unwilling to disturb a great peace. Along the road, emptiness, except for a visionary sentry motionless, like a statue or a tree-stump frozen into harmony with the surroundings: several ghosts were bending and rising to the right, a working-party laying out wire. They seemed to be digging their own grave.

In that junction of mysterious man and nature rests the unique interest of this type of war, the only feature of a monotonous life. And this junction is not confined to night, but to day also: men living and working on a hill-side so completely screened by adaptive colour that only movement betrays; a deserted village housing unnoticed a whole brigade, or even half a division; or a farm-house, almost completely ruined, covering a company. Trenches may be occupied in daylight by a battalion marching along sunken roads for miles, or through communication trenches, and the observer may look across country, see nothing whatever, and report no movement anywhere.

But the land is so flat, so unlike my own country. Even if it had the joy of murmurous existence, a patter of tongues and feet, voices of men and children along busy roads, under shadowy eaves vibrating with hidden life; even if it were a hive of subdued activities and a home of happy domesticity, the hills are not striding across, and their breath does not sweep it. I was reading Buchan's *Salute to Adventurers* when I met this passage : " And I ", said Elspeth, " would be threading rowan berries for a necklace in the heather of Medwynglen. It must be about four o'clock of a midsummer afternoon, and a cloudless sky, except for white streamers over Tinto. Ah ! my own kind countryside ". You know the sudden sickness that comes when the old place glides into vision again and there is no possibility of satisfying desire. Buchan sums up the beauty I liked above all, a cloudless sky beyond Tinto, when the Pentland hills and Tweeddale glimmer and darken to jewelled turquoise, catching a primrose cloud and tossing it from peak to peak until the lower sky gleams emerald and distance is a wonderfully delicate gradation of lemon and gold. There is no such gliding of fine colour to a finer horizon here, but a sudden fall of cloud before a ridge.

Like the others, I have learned to gourmandize on a sprat, and find a day's contentment in a mere shadow of comfort. I can believe myself on Sandilands Moor when I read Dumas's lines :—

Mais tout cela ne vaut pas l'air des vastes campagnes
Et les chansons du soir dans le fond des bosquets.

.   .   .   .   .

I am beginning to understand from my own experience the miseries of Grimmelshausen's *Simplicissimus*, who could catch lice in handfuls. Here we scratch all day and all night, or sit like rabbits in front of our warren examining shirts. A facetious gentleman termed it " hunting on the lawn ". A great and lasting benefit of trench-life, just like living in a marble palace attended by devoted slaves ! It arouses wonder and develops philosophy. Diogenes had a real martyr's life in a barrel : on the bare ground the lice are legion, inside anything comfortable they surpass in number the sands on the shore.

I have taken a new interest in beetles, especially when wakened at midnight by an inquisitive gentleman exploring my chest. They crawl up and down the walls of the dug-out, strange jet monsters dear to Scarabeaus, shaped to inspire terror in a child soul. Caterpillars are very constant with their attentions, dear little playfellows escorted by earwigs and huge spiders. Ladybirds preen themselves on your knees and go to sleep in boots ; ants delight to scamper up one leg and down the other, get lost sometimes and emerge at your neck in a great state of bewilderment. Greenflies and bluebottles utter dulcet melody all day long, strange buzzers hover on the face and tickle the ears and nostrils. There is a constant interchange of courtesies between the grasshoppers on the banks, and crickets rattle lugubriously by the road-side at night.

Strange bedfellows always seem the most romantic, and we have enough of them here to inspire a new kind of epic :—

Sweet to me, O ant, are thine eyes in the morning,
Gazing calmly at me from the promontory nose,
And thy shaggy hair rustles delightfully o'er me
Like wind on the plains tressing the corn.

Then the poet could continue and string a lot of beautiful images round this fairy-like Shakespeare with Queen Mab, touching the sublime a little and avoiding the trivial as not in keeping with this great subject. I can see Virgil becoming jealous and Æneas fading away to a very shadowy character indeed beside this wonderful creation.

. . . . .

"It is romance that holds the two-edged sword, the sharp ecstasy and the severing scythe stroke, the expectancy and the disillusioning, the trance and the clearer vision" (*Some Irish Yesterdays*). If one could govern life, feeling, perception, spirit, desire, experience, to that definition, the old feeling of Paradise would appear tame beside the most ordinary, and the richest delight of existence or nature gleam eternally on the deserted and desolate. Sometime it might come to me and make me forget those things, holding the vision to the rainbow at the world's end and leading, as it led Ralph in *The Wood Beyond the World*, through pain, temptation, misery, voluptuous crime, to a quiet world, peaceful in a pure happiness, settled at last in a great consummation.

"Ainsi l'homme est si malheureux qu'il s'ennuierait même sans aucune cause d'ennui, par l'état propre de sa complexion : et il est si vain qu'étant plein de mille causes essentielles d'ennui, la moindre chose, comme un ballon ou une balle qu'il pousse, suffit pour le divertir " (Pascal). Pascal got the idea all right. The least thing delights us here, and the only sop to weariness is a constant expectation of meeting little things out of the ordinary, things no one else might notice but are all the world to us.

HERMIES,
16 August, 1917

The *Literary Supplement* was to me as a warmth-giving tonic, especially when the thought comes that perhaps the old life of ruminating among books and among past pictures, memorials of past centuries, will be difficult of reattainment, and that this may be one of the means of keeping in touch and not entirely forgetting that peculiar beauty or flavour of a more cultured world. It seems so strange writing thus in this desolation. Even now, in the open, away from the heavy atmosphere of the dug-out, a rat scampers across the path and disappears beneath a sheet of corrugated-iron.

The Army does not study individualities, but it has indulged a fondness of mine. We have a unique opportunity of viewing sunrise and sunset in the trenches owing to the decree that men must stand-to at daybreak and nightfall. Perhaps without this one would forget or lack resolution to study the sky on one's own initiative. I have felt sometimes that there was nothing really worth while, and lethargy overtook me when one of those far-flung sunsets flaming over the hill reminded me that I had something more to live for than sleep in a muddy trench, that the everlasting beauty was still alive, even when least suspected.

Dante, the all-adaptable, gives his utterance:—

> Ciò chè vedeste fu, perche non scuse
> D'aprir lo core all' acqua della pace
> Chè dall' eterno fonte son diffuse.

A noble thought!

Laying a broad tapestry of happiness in resignation visualized for ever, that quiet unaffected subservience of self to the need for spiritual calm, the tone of a single endeavour ringing clear through trial. The gloomiest perspectives have that silver line running through them, and tracing a path from their desolation to the broader fields of an Elysian beauty, Arcady become spiritualized, and its shepherds and shepherdesses grown into earnest humans. I think it the finest religion of all, that, even on the grey battlefield, the great wings are swooping and the great heart absorbing its horror into beauty, touching the heart and soul with its new-found grace and teaching them to throw aside the sordid to concentrate on the essential. Not religion de-Christianized, but morality fined down to something more radiant than religion.

.   .   .   .   .

I have wandered somewhat from the first intention, of describing cloud-life viewed at rise and fall. Even this morning the sun has stolen like a lance along the ridges and beneath the trees, cutting adrift the white mist hanging over them, and sprinkling the lower sky with filmy blue. The clouds mount above it in a beautiful mackerel; their wings are broadened for flight, pearl-lights dwelling in the hollows and opal shadows, like an army of angels fleeing from night to day. I have never seen such glorious vistas of sunset or sunrise as in this country. Its flatness gathers up everything to the world overhead and adds a great depth and shimmering distance to the gold, rose, and green, touching them finely to delicate gleam. Sunrise remains a definite beauty of glowing colour wandering over the sea of air through clouds—not a memory called from books and accepted for fashion's sake.

Strange that this should be the whole of life, yet how satisfying it is! The mind or memory cannot turn its full face to the materials of war and forget all else: once a dug-out is made or a trench hollowed out, then they are as if they had never been. As in an obstacle race, buoyant hope leaps over them all and stays only at the consummation, seeing the end even through a wilderness of obstructions. That is my idea: perhaps there exists some who can find a lifetime's vocation in shouldering duckboards, coils of barbed wire, sheets of iron, etc.; cul-de-sac souls who are content with little, and are never really happy. This philosophy can be defined in the Psalmist's words: " He who regardeth the clouds shall not sow ".

We are busy cutting a road for transport between two high banks. To-day the " pleinairiste " would be delighted with the ensemble: sun glistening on dry earth-heaps, and men, recumbent, shading eyes from the glare. There are only two colours, light purple and dark blue-grey; the purple grows warm and luminous, living as a reflection on water, and the shadowed faces shine nevertheless transparently, with a mat light along nose and eyes, just sketching the features. Laura Knight could make a delightful tableau, just a touch here and there to raise the figures of men and tools above the prevailing light and suggest overwhelming floods of shimmering colour, burning and blazing whitely in the sun. Even dark objects—boots or equipment—are bathed in the luminance and lose contrast to become merged in the whole. The heat is so great that no real light and shadow remain, just a difference of form, not of colour, shadows clearly projected but not salient. The sky comes forward over the hill, not the infinite azure sea, where clouds float at a vast distance, but a fine blue screen with white patches of cumuli rising slowly to the zenith.

Strange flies, born of the sun, flit along the path; huge bees whizz past uncannily; butterflies rise and settle again on the hot clay; there is a multitude of greenflies and bluebottles buzzing noisily in the shadows. There dwells a fineness in it all, a sultry beauty of contour untouched by association. Just before me a figure sits in the doorway, silhouetted against the purplish glare, every line of him clean, sharp, and beautiful, with a reflected silver on cheek and nose, bent arm and knee. Just a fine cameo of grey colour drawn in arabesque of perfect line.

HERMIES,
19 August, 1917

I had my first real experience of a bombardment last night in an observation-post just opposite Havrincourt. "Minenwerfer" and whizzbangs were dropping all round me, bursting redly in the long grass and crashing on the sunless road beneath. The characteristic of a whizzbang is its speed: the victim has no time to estimate his chances before the shell is on him. It travels as swift as sound, with the result that the bang of the gun coincides with the explosion. I was wondering which one would get me next, but the enemy found it impossible to get anything like a direct hit. One, however, covered me with dirt and gave me a nice hour's work shaking shirt and trousers clear.

If you are in a mood for fireworks and artificial illumination, the scene last night would have satisfied your wildest expectations. The brigade to the right of us put over liquid-fire and shell-gas. I was dreaming comfortably at my post, watching thistle-heads bob up and down and rats trip lightly over the sandbags when a sudden flare on the opposite ridge wakened me to reality. A long, low bank of white smoke became visible in front of a yellow starlight thrown up from the enemy lines; then it swelled out, rose on end, trailed off in long tails, and at last rolled across in an overwhelming wave, burning like slag fresh from the furnace. Meanwhile green lights were rising to the right and left, showers of stars trailed in a long arc and fell into the white wave, flying darts rose and flickered, and occasionally a red light showed that the enemy craved the help of artillery.

The volume of smoke increased and blotted out even the highest Vèry lights, so that the illumination appeared to come from behind instead of within: to the left a broad yellow flare shone dimly, like an October moon rising from mist on the fields. Rising and falling, the great wave swept over Cambrai and beyond, forming of sky, valley, hill, a strangely gradated monotone in every shade of green—green of the first leaf and green of the deepest pool.

The noise was terrific: gas-shells, trench-mortars, " flying-pigs ", " minenwerfers ", 9·2's, 18-pounders, whizzbangs—all crashing

THE SOMME

together ; machine-guns kept rattling away from both lines. Strange to say, the German artillery did not reply until an hour afterwards, when the bombardment I have mentioned began. Even in the darkness the bank of gas gleamed obscurely for miles, like a cloud lying along the horizon.

The effect appeared the most magnificent I have ever seen, even in imagination : the idea that so many lives perished in the smoke added a certain solemnity to the picture, not perhaps in the wave itself, nor in the flash and flare of light, but in the colouring thought. Even the slightest thing that tells of human struggle or pain becomes ennobled in self, and perhaps more sublime. That is my idea of last night.

.   .   .   .   .

Above me German anti-aircraft shells are bursting in the azure. Some of our aeroplanes come past regularly every evening, and the same welcome meets them. The conies come forth from their holes and gaze heavenward, like the Wise Men following a star. The air seems full to satiety with humming, distant and near, as if thousands of bees had deserted the flowers and sought a new nectar in the clouds.

There is something wonderfully picturesque in the life. Two nights ago, while heaving up earth, I saw what resembled a piece of phosphorus lying at my feet. I stooped down and picked it up. When it began to squirm and wriggle over my hand, I knew it was a glow-worm, and digging took on interest. Henceforth my concern was to uncover glow-worms, not to pile up a parapet.

Apart from their beauty, association makes them precious. I remembered Shelley's lines in the *Skylark*.

>Like a glow-worm golden in a dell of dew.

The antiquarian imagination raised that humble creature lying quiescent on the ground into the scope of fine imagery and broad-winged thought, touching it to the angel and poising it above the sordid. For the moment I forgot I was in the war, and not in the grasp of romance centred in narrative, alive in fiction. Then some one ventured the humorous remark, the enemy had sent up a great number of Very lights that night. Of course, he meant the stars.

.   .   .   .   .

In Billets.

A romantic gentleman has just joined our platoon, a Highlander of Highlanders, fresh from the Old Country. On Friday evening I was lying back reading Dante when I heard a " glou-glou " of subdued music. In the distance, sitting on the edge of his bed, our friend played a chanter of peculiarly low pitch. All I could see was a white gleam of hand going up and down, a nose and towsy mass of hair speckled with light. A real clansman, speaking English with difficulty and filled with stories of his great father, the piper " par excellence ", who had taught him all the chants worthy of his home. He rendered the common, well-known clan-songs, dances, pibrochs, in a dropping of murmurous notes, like water falling to a pool. The most delicious melody I have heard, not by sheer beauty of sound, but by the suggestive lack of emphasis. The dreamer had room to dream while it went on, and the spirit had inspiration to create a world around that play of wavering note. Yesterday he was brimful of anecdote of life among the Cuchullin Hills of Skye, days spent at nothing else but lying on heather watching white cloud and distant sea.

HERMIES,
21 August, 1917

I wonder whether God has created this weather to show a more transcending mercy than heretofore, that a perfect day of sun can coincide with war and decide a beauty of its own. Last night and this morning!

After all, there rests some pleasure in life when two such harmonies of lovely colour and light float into vision and raise an enchanting face. The hollow road runs north and south, so that the rising sun measures off a gradation of gleam and shadow on the one side and the setting on the other. Two ladders of descending and ascending loveliness! Below the sun-line a misty grey rounds off the edges of the corners, dwells in the hollows, and lingers on the road. The shed supports are bi-coloured—gold and pearl—and the stacks of boards, wire, iron, draw on the earthen wall a clearly outlined shadow, like an Assyrian picture. Then, above the line, what an overflow of dancing light! Light in the earth shadow and the grass, light in the fields and broad sky so that the infinite seems to have descended to earth and embraced in a caress as infinite.

A khaki-clad officer comes down, half in

shadow, half in sun. His feet move in a subdued twilight, while his head and shoulders are bathed in the gold. Cloverheads and thistles, in silhouette yet illuminated, hang drowsily their heads, uncertain of life and uncertain of light, mingling leaf and flower in a warm grey which gives a finer beauty to the dreamy azure overhead.

Then, last night, what a glory of haunting illumination was there! The clouds had passed in a flurry of rose from the sky and left a subtle gradation of pure colour from zenith to horizon, hovering and smiling in a thousand shimmering lights. It passed from the loveliest purple to a warm orange, through lilac, pale turquoise, amethyst, rose, pearl-grey, lemon, and gold, like one of those evening skies Stott paints to bathe an ordinary group of men or animals in a mysterious half-light, not dream and yet not reality.

Shadows slept in the road, blue as a sunlit sea and transparent as fine glass; above them the sun laid a long tapestry of orange, against which the grass tufts told startlingly. Men walking below had face and breast illuminated crudely, like figures in an impressionistic fresco—yellow features, outlined with dark-blue shadow. Yet with that, depth was in the air, a bottomless sea of beauty, where all thought of pain and yearning swam away in infinite peace, and the only reality of life was a sinking in it, a fortunate shipwreck, and the abiding truth came as vision, the chaste vision of an infinite harmony.

Sound gave utterance to the joy of earth: beetles, droning in a curious bass tone that rang everywhere, flew from one bank-head to another; there was a constant buzzing of flies in the damp hollows, murmurous in distance; and overhead the sky echoed humming of invisible aeroplanes.

Not a shell burst anywhere. Only in the sky a few balls of white smoke from anti-aircraft shells became tenuous and gradually faded away. Calm on the earth and calm in sky! If there were calm in the world what a reward that would be, a renewed hope in an eternal rule, a new eye for the eternal beauty, and a sure faith through experience in an eternal kindness.

The night was a lyric in itself; one of those magic soul-gleams that come but rarely to man, and are a constant attribute of harmony between sky and earth. Murmur, dream, and loveliness—all three rising and falling in perfect rhythm as the queen's cloak when at the last she will throw aside the shuttle, and instead of weaving tapestries of divine beauty, will come across to vision, will come to rejoice the spirit with the long-sought beauty which is eternity in self and perfect grace.

> The murmurous haunt of flies on summer eves.

Keats had his moment of surrender and gave utterance to the inner need. But if his words are lovely, they do nought but hint at the reality. Throned in the absolute such visions can only receive imperfect recognition and halting reproduction. The human has only a glimpse, and his picture remains incomplete.

AN ORCHARD IN VELU,
24 August, 1917

I found a German soldier's diary in a rubbish-heap, an interesting relic of a life, past perhaps, which tells of an intimacy of friendship near to tears, something sacred between spirit and spirit which shrinks from the spoliator. A loving son, evidently, and a fine husband, newly married, he talks with evident delight of his bride, and gives a very careful address written in beautiful script. A native of Saxony, he kept a note of letters and field postcards written during the months from September 1916 to April of this year. His bride's address is given :—

> Fräulein Anna Schmeder,
>   in Kuppelsdorf Post Dahwe,
>   Bei Schweinitz,
>   Provinz Sachsen,

and his own :—

> Paul Schmaun,
>   Ruh Depot der 7 Fusz Kamp,
>   Feldpoststatten,
>   Belgien.

His letter written in case of accident runs :—

Liebe Kamaraden Sollte ich irgend verwundet oder den Heldentod fürs Vaterland sterben, so bitte ich denjenigen, der mir findet, sofort meine Angehörigen bescheid.

His greatest output of letters took place in March, seventeen letters and six cards. I think I have written more myself, but not being methodical like our Saxon hero, I can't count any of them. Another lady's address was :—

> Frau Witwe Anna Schröder,
>   Diesdorf bei Magdeburg,
>   2 Mittelstrasse.

This lady wanted to convey her kind regards, a widow apparently. This she did through his mother.

Quite a unique thing, isn't it ? Not complex, but very suggestive, telling of a home-life like our own with as strong affections.

III

FLANDERS

BERTINCOURT,
27 August, 1917

I AM inclined to think you are causing yourself too much discomfort about me. After all, the worse I can get just now goes to a hardening. All I want you to consider is this : that so far I have told the unvarnished truth, coloured bareness in places, given sordid things a new gleam which might enliven them to my idea, but make them more squalid still perhaps to yours, but I have never consciously said things were well with me when they were not. It might sound harsh to your ear at the time, weak, nostalgic, but nothing loses in repetition, and if pleasure comes and I say so, then you can believe me to your heart's content and not be deceived. Thus I don't want you to lay too much stress on any sickness you think to find in my letters ; it is a mood rather than a condition, wears off in a minute and may be replaced by an intense momentary delight.

Some write letters as a mere formality, not too careful about facts, and always insisting on the top note, like a mavis on a spring morning. One could easily say: " I am in the pink ", etc., in every screed, but what's the good of that ? That has no value to anybody, least of all to the man who writes it. A letter, as I conceive it, is at best a picture, not drawn with pencil or brush, but a picture for all that of the writer, and as such should be inherently true. The more vivid the description of moods and fancies, the better and more valuable it is. Even if I don't wish you to think of me as one who goes singing *Cherry Bright* with an easy conscience always, I don't wish you to see me brooding or melancholic.

So far, war has remained a romance to me; every page, every incident, a part of a definite purpose, clear design. If you could look at it like that and treat everything that happens calmly, dispassionately, knowing the end of the story will be the end of fairy, " and they lived happily ever afterwards ", we would surely have a good time, making pleasant adventures out of passing troubles, and join disgust, despair, boredom, with delight, joy, and interest to form a real happiness. I look on it that way, prepared for anything and surprised at nothing, certain of clearing a path through every obstacle and of " getting there " in the long run.

I know it is an ideal hard to accomplish, and even harder to seek, making a letter a part of myself, but if you can even hear me speaking, however faintly and distantly, as I can with yours, then it will be crowned with success and find ample justification. You must be cheerful at all times : even if fatalist, one can be an optimist as well. The new rendering is " Everything comes to those who know how to wait ". If I can keep patience, the cards will fall to me soon and give me a winning hand. I am sure of that as I am that this beautiful day of sunshine has come after a wet night, and the white clouds moving royally across the blue are the aftermath of a great storm of wind and rain.

. . . . .

COURCELLES-LE-COMTE,
2 September, 1917

One can never decide definitely about anything there ; there is no time, even for decent, thinking ; always on the move should be our war-cry. I have seen a vast chunk of France now and I don't feel inclined to enthuse about its beauty, the same monotony of streamless plains. A new brand of nostalgia enters the system: one longs for a purling brook, a clear lake, and a whole village. I have seen enough ruins to send our feather-brained sentimentalists into the last stages of delirium.

I am beginning to overcome the lice nuisance. This week I had a slight dose of influenza, but got over it without after-effects. Too close to the ground! I wonder how the poor idealist would look, picturing a starry world of imagery across the roof of a dug-out. How delicious it would be to have a crisp, clean walk across-country and get rid of the rubbish in the system! A breath of the pure air about Tinto would be worth an infinity of lime-juice drinks, but then, Tinto has faded away back into Elysium, and the wanderer would have to sprout wings to reach his desire.

A treasure, the *Mirror of the Sea*! Did you notice Conrad's description of the West Wind? Fine! I read it with as much deliberate pleasure as a connoisseur tasting good wine. Not the swift piling-up of heavy imagery, and words to a powerful conclusion, as in Ruskin, but a nice completion of pictures to form one picture. It reminded me of a slow, quiet trickle of water through fern to a fall on rotten leaves, drop by drop, delicately musical. I like good English at all times (our padre's designation of some men being "in love with avoirdupois"), but when dished out so delicately and richly, just to suit a cloyed palate, it becomes more luscious than a feast of peaches. I have no more to say on that subject at present; don't want to get muddled up with my own conceits, like a belated Euphuist.

For a perfect idea of a French farm-house in our district I would like you to look at L'Hermitte's *Pay-Day*. Just now I am reading Vernon Lee's *In Praise of Old Houses* (Longmans, 1892), found in the padre's reading-room. The Epicurean idea is the best: make the most of a good thing when you have it and let the future go to the devil. In fact, a Stoic-Epicurean would have a glorious time just now, and the old Cynic antagonist fill the trenches to every one's satisfaction; but the doubt arises, would he do for fighting? Too canny, perhaps; too bald in his perception of facts. The barbarian is the darkest fighter after all;

he goes right at it, sinks his teeth in an opponent's throat or get his own jugular severed.

The moderns do not worship the man of action as much as the man of ostentation. I have heard some of our men telling how such and such a man does a lot without saying much: such men fulfil the latter qualification to the letter, but the doing lies in a very remote future. If, like Wells's hero, they sit in profile like saints cut in alabaster, they have every chance of getting a real statue erected. "To the Memory of ―――― for Conspicuous Bravery" is not so bad a heading after all, though our plain common-sense English has not the sonorous weight of "Hier ruht Unteroffizier Elble, gefallen für Vaterland".

.   .   .   .   .

I noticed a remark by Vernon Lee, quoting some one, "That the action of time makes man's works into natural objects." I only wish it were really true; then squalor of ruins and sordidness of decay would become a thing of beauty, a base for the fine flower and the stately tree, for the waving grass and an infinity of happy life, taking up existence and passing into oblivion in a quietness of natural function.

The village where we stay illustrates the opposite of that remark. The country, as far as eye can see, is bare except for a tree or two dotted along the roads. All the winds of heaven touch it, for now it lies in an exposed place. The Germans drilled holes in the trees and exploded them into long splinters, making a complete desert. Yet the old-time peasant, with that primitive instinct for shelter which gives our Army faith in the immunity of ramshackle dug-outs, chose it as a site: the trees were higher, the foliage thicker, the coppice denser, and the grass longer. The thick leaves tempered the harsh wind (for the winds are cold here at all times): the coppice was hollowed out, bushes and fruit trees planted—pears, apples, damsons, red currants—the grass divided into grazing ground, where the tethered cows ate their fill. This done and the red-tiled cottages erected, religion claimed the next duty. This took concrete shape in a huge square building of chalk-slabs, painted inside with all manner of symbol and picture of the Virgin Mary. Even in ruin there is to the left of the chancel a Botticelli-like *Mother and Child* surrounded by a filigree of texts as " Qui prie se sauve " and sketches of incidents in the life of Jesus.

This might appear a bald narration, " House-that-Jack-built " type, but it holds something wonderfully interesting. It came home to me last night when I saw a glorious sunset flushing the face of the sky to blood-red, too red to be painted, for the artist would have been accused of hard colour. Not a movement in the leagues of green meadow-land or in the village : trees, bushes, houses, gleamed nothing but bones—bones of a body whose soul had gone and might never be renewed.

Yet the French have begun to plough up the land with motor-tractors : just across the valley lies a long wood in front of which stretch acres of ploughed turf waving and winding to indefinite distance where the Aisne comes through a broad depression. The enemy retired with such haste that he never cut down the orchards hidden in that wood by Ablainzeville : beautiful orchards, too, with rosy fruit strung as thickly as beads along the branches—damsons in thick clusters, pear-espaliers rising above a wilderness of nettles, apples of every variety from a grey, perfectly-formed russet to a soft juicy cider. I won't forget that quiet village in its nest of tall trees, vaguely splendid as a dream : high poplars by white roads, with a pale sky behind them, as if Corot had planted them there to please a fine instinct ; vaguely glimmering châteaux in the shadow of foliage, where a dog's barking sounds at intervals ; romantic houses, where groups of "poilus" gather round a broad table, talking all day while the wine goes round. There was a churchyard, where our dead and the Germans slept side by side. I was brooding sadly before a finely executed memorial to an airman, broad wings rising from an urn of granite, when a French soldier interrupted me. He showed me the graves of French and British officers crowned with headstones executed by the Germans as a mark of veneration, and a lonely mound in a corner glorious with the tricolour, where a " poilu " had died in 1914. Perhaps when the war has finished, we won't grudge to our enemies that deed of pity or that kindness. The gates to the cemetery were intact, delicately designed ironwork hanging from two white pillars.

Beyond the wood lay another village—Achiet-le-Petit—just ruined enough to be uninhabitable, and on the other side a deep valley, so steep that it became a matter of mystery why the Germans did not make a stand on the other side. Shell-holes clustered at the bottom, dried up or filled with water, where a million animalculæ swarmed: not a tree was visible anywhere, yet such a perfect gradation of soft greys from rose to pale blue as I have never seen or even dreamt. We seemed to enter a dim world of fairy, grey warriors going into a new Valhalla, where all harshness and ruggedness had been smoothed down into quiet loveliness, and a peaceful contentment taken the place of violent action; where the spirit could forget yearning and find its faintest desires broaden out into a graciousness as if heaven were earth, and earth a kindlier God. It was morning, morning in full summer, when we went there, and a veil of rose lay over the earth, touching a far town—Achiet-le-Grand—to a golden mystery of wall and tree, and outlining with silver the broad road that led from it in the direction of Bapaume.

.   .   .   .   .

I have lost all taste for pure landscape, taken such a horror of lifeless fields, deserted roads, empty houses, where even nature has left passion to die and passivity of coming death overtakes all, that even the happiest and most peaceful beauty of flowery meadow and dark grove will seem ineffectual without a human figure moving in it. The critic could pull me up for that, a recession to the old Victorian idyll stage, when no country walk was complete without two lovers mooning about like wingless bats. The war will stop that nonsense or encourage it. I am afraid it will encourage sentimentality. Life in the trenches does not make for fine taste in the arts. Something coarser in fibre, something more obvious appeals to us, something that will strike the eye and heart with resounding effect. If a picture looks like a design for wall-paper, then it will remain so : the simple, dear things will carry off the prize. The purely romantic should receive a welcome of relief, a dispelling of past agony by a more beloved picture.

Of course, we have still the great comfort, " Truly the light is sweet and a pleasant thing it is to see the sun ". The airs play around us and whisper promise ; colour moves in the cloud and rests in the clear sky, wakes to beauty in the morning and dies to glory at night ; even if the birds are silent and only swallows, magpies, and bats flit about, the grasshoppers and the crickets discourse from dawn to dawn. Small things, small sufficiencies ! Even then, we haven't lost everything : memory rebuilds the hearthstone on the hearth, sets up four walls again and furnishes the mansion. More beautifully, perhaps, than ever in reality!

"I remember walking thus along the bastions under the bishop's palace at Laon, the great stone cows peering down from the belfrey above, with a sense of irrepressible familiarity and peace." This sentence of Vernon Lee rings strange now: I think feeling will be opposite, and the stone cows will have gone to ruin, like good things. But our army might march into it this year, and we shall see for ourselves.

COURCELLES-LE-COMTE,
8 September, 1917

Indigestion is troubling the battalion at the present hour. One day we scouted down a flat valley bottom, along a tree-shadowed road, across a spare wood, to a square copse. In the wood, an orchard of rosy crab-apples was discovered. We spent an hour replenishing stomachs and filling balmorals with the sweet, acrid fruit, and lay in a shallow trench sunning ourselves for an afternoon. From that time there has been a constant succession of fruit-patrols to all parts of the compass, each armed with a sandbag, which is always filled either with apples or pears. The child-natural element revives in war: prejudices, social veneers, little delicacies of taste and manner of life, choice actions dictated by a particular regard to decorum, become merged in a quiet comfort-seeking in the slightest gift, even a crab-tree studded with minute apples.

A morning-wash in the green water of a shell-hole, a thankful moistening of lips in a vile water drawn from a chlorinated tank, an attempt at china-cleaning by a handful of dewy grass, a sharpening of razors on a rifle-sling show how casual is the whole business. I have admired a fine sunrise between my legs as I bent over a shallow dish of muddy liquid to wash a grey physiognomy. If everything were cut and carved, measured out nicely for us, and arranged to suit, lethargy would overcome us (it does set in, in a most deadly fashion, and one of war's worst hardships is to defeat it) and we would be a sorry set of lifeless automatons. There is such a wealth of insect life on French soil that no one lies long on grass without being uncomfortable. A long afternoon's sleep in the sun appears to my mind entirely out of the question, and the best one can do is to peer out the printed page in a semi-obscure billet.

This morning was dreamy with mist. An incessant low-toned pattering of drops from the trees gave it a voice, an utterance strangely at variance with the booming of trench-mortars practising in the vicinity. The landscape died away to dim milky shadows vaguely suggested; only a pair of wheels painted green, astride a trench, lent detail. At the top of an elm a jay was cracking uncertainly, dreaming still of warm nights; then, impatient of my examination, flew away, with long tail shaking, like a wagtail grown gigantic. A frail beauty dwelt there: tall trees with the foliage gleaming a pale note of colour, wild grass with heads grown filmy in suspended shadow, hedges a bar of opal across the tree-trunks, long, low valleys a woolly swathed indefiniteness, vaguely smiling with the promise of sun, and above all a great bowl of sky, flashing with an infinity of subdued tints and gracious veiled forms. Like a drawing of Raphael's, the more intently it was viewed the finer became the lines, and the shadows more tender, until its loveliness gleamed exquisite as a dream. No clear colour anywhere, no broad glintings, but a soft diffusion of opal light resting lightly on the high places and brooding in a tenuous shadow, background for a fine conception.

COURCELLES-LE-COMTE,
12 September, 1917

This morning the Colonel summoned the whole battalion to the concert-hall, a ruined house with a roof of yellow tarpaulin. We knew perfectly well what was coming. A fortnight's training in bombing, firing of rifle-grenades, shooting at disappearing targets, and practise of assault-formations going in waves over a hill, gave us an inkling of hot work in front of us. He told us of the traditions the division stood for, the high position it held in the regard of the Army Commander, appealed to the courage of an army which had triumphed at Messines, Vimy, Arras, and Ypres ; recalled to us the German treatment of our prisoners, and of harmless Belgian and French civilians, violation, seduction, murder, until it appeared a sacred duty to die fighting in such a cause. At the last he warned us solemnly of the penalties attached to cowardice in the field. " If the Hun shells too heavily, side-slip, but for God's sake don't go back. We have him by the short hairs, and it only remains for us to make a finished job. We have all had a fierce time punishing him and making him pay for those desecrations of human hearths and hearts ; by the grace of God, we shall give him so much of his own hell that he will wish he had never created such misery. Do not shoot prisoners when such—that is, murder on his own lines ; do not kill wounded if they are in desperate condition and helpless. If prisoners are in your way, you are allowed to dispose of them as you please. Not otherwise ! "

When he had finished and we went out into the clear air, into the quietly smiling sunlight, a feeling not exactly of pain or even fear overtook me : a dim sense of exaltation, as if a definite vocation in life had been assured, a definite reward, a final gathering of all forces of soul and will to answer a great call, an obliteration of every quavering and hesitation, as if the new quest was nobler than that legendary one of Parzival. This was the real thing at last, not a mere toying with life and fate. The balance would be decided between life and death—death with no lingering and in a full glory of achievement, life after a stern battling with danger and crowned with joy in the thought of courage proved. I think the real religion must be a development of that uncertain exaltation, a strange concurrence in the unseen and perhaps inevitable, a definite view of soul across a broad world of shadow, a surrender to the great power we call God, accomplished in silence and received in silence. Nobility of presence suggested by an uplift of desire, by a stirring of the deeper conscience, not a folding of hands nor a stereotyped mouthing of conventional prayer, but a direct communion. In such a time we are all believers, cannot help it. There is need of sympathy and sustenance, of belief in a certain mission and of reward for play with death, and that is the spirit's will and way.

The afternoon appeared in a new glory, and the white clouds, travelling in flocks across a diaper of shadow and silver gleam, held a vague promise as if they were then creations of another will smiling down, draped in a glory of life, and visualized in a mood of kindness. They were as truly alive as we, and in them, in the tall pillared trees, in the flower-covered gardens and ruined houses, in the distant plains, and in the immense depth of shimmering air overhead, the vague longings were quieted and the spirit felt at one with a great spirit, junction of soul to soul.

"And perhaps a very great and painful effort which you are not disposed to make ; but this is a world of effort, you know." I have a vague idea Dickens wrote this : I can only hope this effort we must make will be successful, and that its fruit will be lasting and our period of struggle shortened. Even we, even so !

VLAMERTINGHE,
17 September, 1917

You will have read of Belgium in every newspaper dispatch and every book written on war. The best I can do is simply to tell you what I experienced—and suffered more or less patiently. The country resembles a sewage-heap more than anything else, pitted with shell-holes of every conceivable size, and filled to the brim with green, slimy water, above which a blackened arm or leg might project. It becomes a matter of great skill picking a way across such a network of death-traps, for drowning is almost certain in one of them. I remember a run I had at the beginning of this week—for dear life, if you like. Five of us had spent the night patrolling and were returning to Brigade H.Q. when the enemy sighted us and put a barrage along the duckboard track we were following. Early dawn broke in the east, and a grey light filtered eerily through dim cloud-masses to a desolate world of brown, touching the skeleton woods strangely, and blackening the edge of ridge where the German trenches lay. First one shell dropped ten yards behind us, then one came screaming so close that we dropped in our tracks and waited for the end. I got right under the duckboard track, and the hail of shrapnel and mud on it was thunderous enough to frighten the most courageous. Then we stood up, all safe though muddy, and with a " Run like hell, boys ", went off in a devil's race, with shells bursting at our heels, for half a mile, dropping at last in complete exhaustion in a trench out of range.

It is quite the usual thing to stand about a hundred yards away and see some poor devils getting chased for their lives. Our artillery has an interesting habit of putting up a specially warm barrage when the line is being relieved, with the result we get a very thorough shelling in return just when we cannot shelter. When we left the Menin Road and took to the duckboards at a time when the enemy places a barrage on them, the most careless of us cursed the man in front of him if he happened to pause a minute. It seemed the best solace for excited nerves to keep going, no matter whether into or out of danger. Yet, luck stood by us; in spite of our over-zealous artillery, not a shell dropped near us until we reached our trenches, and then we had it stiff. A sergeant and two privates were blown to pieces twenty yards from me: all that night and early morning we lay in the shallow trench, trying vainly to keep knees from shaking and teeth from chattering, with a deadly sick feeling in the stomach as bits of shrapnel hit the side of the trench with a dull thud and earth was shaken over our face. In the morning, through a glorious clear sky of pale blue, we watched our own aeroplanes and the enemy's circling slowly and dropping outside our range of vision, heard the constant rattle of machine-guns and the crack of high shrapnel, white and black. All we could do was to lie motionless on our back and pray that the enemy had not seen us. I tried to sleep, but nervous excitement kept me awake all day until night, when we dug out a new trench. While plying the spade, I encountered what looked like a branch sticking out of the sand. I hacked and hacked at it until it fell severed, and I was picking it up prior to throwing it over the parapet when a sickness, or rather nausea, came over me. It was a human arm.

That did not complete my experiences that night: about eleven o'clock we set out on patrol, but had to take refuge in a deserted pill-box in No Man's Land because the enemy had sighted us. This pill-box had been used at one time as a charnel-house; it smelt strongly of one and the floor was deep with human bones. From there we watched the Vèry lights flickering outside, and, casting a weird light through the doorway, the red flash of bursting shells. Occasionally a direct hit shook us to the very soul. While sitting there, the odour overcame me and I fainted. Waking up an hour afterwards, I found myself alone, without the faintest idea of my whereabouts, uncertain where the enemy's lines were or my own. Some authors practise the description of fear, but nothing they could do could even faintly realize my state. It went beyond fear, beyond consciousness, a grovelling of the soul itself. For half an hour I stood inside, wondering whether to venture out or stay in at eminent risk of daylight coming to disclose me to the enemy. At last, bravery returned, and I went out only to stumble over a derelict wire a hundred yards farther on, and find my hands clutching at a dead man's face. But on the other side of it lay our trench, and I was able to calm down in readiness for the morning barrage.

Our road to Company H.Q. from Ypres is shown in places by dead men in various postures, here three men lying together, there a dead " Jock " lying across a trench, the only possible bridge, and we had to step on him to get across. The old German front-line, now behind our reserve, must be the most dreadful thing in existence, whether in reality or imagination, a stretch of slimy wicker-work bordering a noisome canal of brown water, where dead men float and fragments of bodies and limbs project hideously, as if in pickle. The remembrance of one attitude will always haunt me, a German doubled up with knees under his chin and hand clutching hair above a face of the ghastliest terror.

Yet my first experience of death was worse than this. Our battalion had entrained almost as far as Ypres, and we rested beside the railway for some time, with the engine standing stationary, sending a high pillar of smoke into the air. I expect the German observation balloons had seen it, for the enemy began to place shells on each side of the railway at regular intervals for about two hundred yards. Of course, we sideslipped until it stopped. Then we began to cross the railway : our two companies had just got over when I heard a scream of a shell. Instantly we got on our noses : I looked up cautiously, just in time to see it explode in a thick mass of the other companies on the railway. The scream of despair and agony was dreadful to hear, men shell-shocked out of reason and others dying of frightful wounds. That shell caused sixty casualities and shook the whole battalion for several days. Even when going through the market-square of Ypres, beneath the yellow flash of great howitzers and the roar of naval guns, we thought shells were bursting among us and looked fearfully at every corner, nerve-shaken and absolutely afraid. The sudden roar of a gun made us start guiltily, half-ashamed, and yet unable to control our agitation. That cry of dying men will ring in my ears a long time after everything else will be forgotten.

They have a curious way of finding direction in Belgium. The landscape has no salient features of its own ; everything blasted to mud—railway embankments, woods, roads confused in shell-holes and mine-craters. Trees are only skeletons, and masses of obscene ruins mark farms or houses. You look in vain for a wood where such is marked on the map. The only way at night is to bend down close to the ground and gaze at the skyline for black shadows of pill-boxes; by those shadows you find your way. Or, to remember a road once shown, the oddest details must be noted—a solitary length of rail or wire, a " dud " shell, three stakes together, a fragmentary hedge, a deserted water-logged trench, dead men lying at various angles, and the position of pill-boxes in relation to the track followed. The most exciting time I spent was in hunting " B " Company Headquarters across this monotony of mud and water. I think I must have visited the whole division before finding it, artillery as well as infantry; had to lie through a pretty fierce barrage, too.

Of course, we had our recompense. It was night when the two of us set out to find our company and midday when we finished. About eleven o'clock we saw a light bobbing up and down to our left, and going down to it met an artillery officer, who, on being asked, directed us in the wrong direction. Being absolutely dying of thirst, we waited till he had gone and then prospected for his dug-out. There, we were almost drunk on soda-water and lemonade, dined royally off his table, and came out better men. Those artillery officers do themselves well: this gentleman owned a dining-room as well as a bedroom.

WINIZEELE,
22 September, 1917

Thank goodness, that's all over. We had practically a walk-over. I shall never forget that afternoon in Ypres, when every officer and man we met asked us how our division did in the attack. I was proud of it, too, in some kind of perverse delight, not keen on fighting, yet glad to be in it. Even then, among all that sordid mass of ruins we call Ypres, memory and recollection have given a romantic aspect, as some monument worthy of valour and enshrined in our deeds, where our bravest fought to the last and never yielded. It may be a cemetery, a horrible cemetery at that, but an air of nobility blows round it yet. The horrible remains a characteristic, instance that story of " Hell's Fire Corner ", where two battalions of an

English regiment lie buried, shelled to death. In Ypres, too, are some billets in cellars (the only safe ones we have), where the rats have become so accustomed to soldiers, and so glutted with their blood, that they won't move out of the way—loathsome, bloated creatures, half-blind and as big as cats.

One episode still gives me a certain pleasure. One morning last week, two of us came down through the morning barrage into the square across the canal. Deadbeat, we asked a policeman where we would get a decent sleep for about three hours. He pointed out to us the old Cloth Hall, and there, beneath that massive tower, so dented and bruised that no more can be destroyed by shells, behind a wall of sandbags, we fell asleep. About nine o'clock I woke up and explored a little: just inside the arch hung a delicately-wrought iron lamp, quite intact, with some fragments of glass still in it, and below, a pair of wooden wheels belonging to an old type of gun. Just beyond lay the ruins of the church, a mere blur of a building. The Cloth Hall seemed to have been so battered that not a single sculptured figure, or shadow of a figure, remained, except one gargoyle at the

FLANDERS

end, which leered down as jauntily as ever. When I come back, this incident will remain one of the treasured memories, something to recount time and again, as happening in a land of horror and dread whence few return, like that country Morris describes in the *Well at the World's End*.

The village we are billeted in just now lies at the top left-hand corner of France, as far as I can see, not exactly in Belgium. We came down in buses along that confused mass of G.S. wagons and gun-limbers which leads from Popheringhe to Ypres : we cannot call it a road, for the road itself is only seen at intervals through that jostling procession of men coming from the line and going up, endless chains of artillery lumbers and ammunition carts, etc. The main trouble is the branches overhead : both sides of the road are lined with trees ; not pruned too scrupulously, with the result that life on the top of a bus consists in bobbing up and down to escape obstreperous twigs. We saw an aeroplane dropping straight down out of the sky to fall sideways on one wing, like a stone. It remained in that position, strangely balanced, with the tail pointed towards the grey clouds. Then, again, an observation-balloon went up in flames, struck by shrapnel, and the observer came down nicely in his parachute. Yet we don't trouble much about things in Belgium : we have all become so accustomed to them.

WINIZEELE,
25 September, 1917

Holding the line is fairly safe, except in a hot corner : but our artillery have the enemy so much on the *qui vive* that hot corners become more their privilege than ours. How he manages to exist at all when a discriminating barrage licks up every yard of ground in his vicinity and over him must be one of the great mysteries of warfare. We can understand partly how he manages from our experience in the outposts, shallow ditches deep enough to allow one to lie flat on the back and not project above the surface. Every morning he puts a barrage on those posts, and there we lie, inwardly quaking, while shells burst behind and before, and bits of shrapnel come down round us with a vicious thud. For a whole week our casualties amounted to four killed, blown to fragments by a 5·9.

However, there is good stuff in him yet !— but I think he is on the down-grade, like a street-singer dressed in a frayed frock-coat and tattered linen. The old glory smacks of him, but it's worn and threadbare. The ideas of conquest and victory may bemuse him and place a narcotic in his soul, thus concealing from him the fact that the hell he once thought to plan for us has been planned most effectually for him. The variety of weapons he uses is bewildering. I have walked along a railroad after a barrage and found the weirdest conglomeration of dud shells—" flying-pigs ", " boches ", " 5·9's ", " pine-apples ", " whizzbangs ", " oil-cans ", etc. Gas-shells lay about just burst at the nose-caps, with the gas oozing out very gradually. I remember one of the type which fell between two branches and lodged in the fork of a tree down the Somme. Every one passing that orchard where the tree stood remarked the sweet smell of fruit, only to discover this dud and very few apples. Beside the shells there were " flying-darts ", gaudy red things, with a long flanged tail to balance (the slightest wound from them is deadly, owing to their being poisoned) ; clumsy pomegranate-shaped bombs with huge four-leafed appendices of no earthly use (to my idea) ; the usual " stick-bombs " in hundreds (I used to alarm the nervy people by unscrewing the tin-can and then pulling the string to set the fuse going); boxes on boxes of machine-gun ammunition and powerful machine-guns with the main parts lacking. Belgium is sown with nothing else but those souvenirs of German occupation, and with them helmets, body-plates, and thigh-protectors of tremendous weight held together with leather straps. I should imagine a German dressed in the armour with that strange helmet would be the image of a Lanzknecht of Wallenstein's time. The armour does not really protect them: I found in a mine-crater two men bayoneted together, a "Cameron," who had been caught in the stomach, and a German in the throat, both locked irrevocably, dead at the same time. Such statues appear frequently: one man told me of two he saw at Beaumont-Hamel, not lying down, but standing up, as if wrought in iron.

Of course, if one dwelt on such horrors any length of time, nervous cowardice would ensue, and the result would be disaster. The main idea is to be an Epicurean, get the sum of enjoyment from the smallest detail, and trust to the general disposition of Fate. I can see her smiling faintly and wearily at us all, wondering who is worth life and who death. Like Coleridge's twain in the *Ancient*

Mariner, the outcome lies in a turn of dice, and yet the result is only rest, or deferred rest, the sum of all endeavour. If he saw so many monuments of youth glowing beneath a calm sky, the old Greek would say, " Eros is dead and there is no more beauty on earth ". But we go on, idealists ever, even if we do not know it or appreciate our ideal, indeterminate Parzivals, and victory flits but vaguely like the Grail, filled with the blood of sacrifice and promising noble gifts.

How I wish such ideas could supplant for a moment home yearnings and make us careless of the future ! Life, after all, is only a combination of chords sounded by home, friends, stages of youth, and education, country and its association : without them we would be mere Hamadryads floating in unsubstantial ether.

.   .   .   .   .

The Canal Bank,
Ypres,
6 October, 1917

I am right in the thick of it again, in this historic place which I shall describe some time. When I think of the glorious weather, sunlight shimmering in a molten sky and slow winds just breathing over the wilderness of shell-holes, it seems so hard throwing it all aside for an uncertain end. Yet it must be done. Perhaps Fate may have some kindness in store for me. Last night I had a strangely poignant dream: I was lying in hospital, trying madly to move my legs, both tied down in splints, and biting my lips to overcome pain coming from the right groin. A comfortable wound might be the outcome of this premonition. Let us hope so: then I can see again the Old Country I had given up for lost, hear the old voices, look at the friendly glad faces.

. . . . .

ZEGGERSKAPPELL,
5 October, 1917

White Heather appealed to me, even if it were only that it described life in Glasgow, the lonely life of lodgings, removed from the crowd and yet in it; where one met it by the causeways and brushed past it in the walk, foreign to its aims and utterances and not entirely at union with self. Even if at that time there were a thousand imaginings, and one could not envisage a clear path to the fountain-head through a maze of divergent paths which promised as many gracious things, the sense lay definite that development was in some one of them. Apprenticeship to a spirit-education of which nature approved ! Grey street, dark skies, streaming window-panes, yellow fog on river and dock, desolation of dreary back-courts and square tenements, sooty glimpses of trees in a melancholy park, chimney-stacks lining a muddy oil-flecked canal, glow of ironworks through a smoky night—these played their part in evolving a definite ideal of beauty, the intense beauty which is distilled from ugliness. Romance was an intimate, Conrad appeared the king of writers—and his world was real. Good sense concurred, the spirit thrilled in sympathy, and the heedless natural striving gleamed rosy beside the ultimate reward. Where is it gone, the glory and the dream ?

Even if, like De Quincey, one took an opiate to still the bitter inner questioning, contented oneself with vision-worlds, dream-men and -women, had unreal adventures in an obscure world of faery, toyed with delicate world-pictures sketched by a tormented spirit, the voice cries more insistently until resolution pales and one can hear an echo : where is the origin of endeavour, where its current, whence its consummation ? There is no answer : the high walls form a *cul-de-sac* where no opening appears to the green earth and blue skies of freedom.

Insufficiency is the final misery. Intellect sleeps. The brain descends to sordid trivialities. All the fine upliftings and impulsive happinesses darken down to despair, freedom becomes depression, and life resumes itself in existence, a bestial thing. Categories are decided by the length of the ears, not by quickness or nervous vitality of intelligence. The day's work becomes a ghastly mockery of thinking about the morrow's rations, and sleep is a futile struggle with implacable parasites.

You might think this stuff bitter as gall, of the melancholy mad type. The weather has given its miserable quota : constant showers from stormy skies veined with orange at the horizon, muddy lanes and a dreary swish of wind through hedges breathe of an autumn already well-advanced. Even the merriest must feel its darkness creeping through his armour; for it is insistent, this claim of a world shedding the glory of a past joyous colour, never certain of a calm, serenely splendid day, never wholly at ease in a cloud.

There is a curious self-containedness in the

life of a French peasant. Even the farm-stock fraternize in a strange way. Yesterday the good wife (who waddles along as if cut through at the waist, bust and hips wobbling in different directions), brought in a cartful of dried bean-stuff. It seemed to be a delicacy, for first a brown cow slipped up and tore off a mouthful, then a calf, then an old grey mare and foal, until the cart was completely surrounded and the old wife lost to view. Quite a fine picture!—cows, horses, a loquacious sow, infinity of white hens, ducks, and, bringing up the rear, a troop of half-grown turkeys.

Last night, at orange afterglow, I saw a wonderfully quiet harmony of greys united in an ancient thatched, mud-walled farmhouse standing above its own reflection in a sheltered pond. Willows bent over the smooth water to shade the more vivid gleam of moss and mould, tracing an arabesque of branch and leaf across the luminous darkness. And the open patches of light, meeting the evening sky, brought gold of a radiant beauty down to their very heart, gold more radiant than had ever appeared to Midas in dream, or Botticelli designing an aureole round a Madonna's head. I could have made a perfect picture drawn wistfully and brushed in colour dreamy enough to visualize that silent beauty : but nothing surely could ever give that repose, that soul-calming sleep of gracious colour, which came like a cooling hand and touched to a peace eternal in scope. An impression, almost a step in history, a mode of comparison, when violence sickens and shock darkens perception !

There are some scenes whose very appearance tells of a long history, of a succession of events sometimes important and epoch-making in a vanished era, but hallowed now by time to a restful memory. That old house, darkened in the subdued light so that all its imperfections were lost in harmony, symbolized a generation of quiet unambitious endeavour, held a whole century of patient, humble peasants, content with the day's work and bringing their vague emotions, unexpressed desires, to the massive chapel just visible beyond the misty woods. If, to come closer to the understanding of the values of life, the people flung aside their long inculcated worship of the Virgin, dismounted those painted porcelain Madonnas fixed to their walls or in lonely shrines by the wayside, desired a symbol more in unison with their life, they could bend their head before that silent beauty of house and water ; contented with the thought that at the last their life would receive a wondering consummation, their vague poetry a definite utterance, and their patient endeavour something of that eternal beauty which hovers over the world.

How quaint their actions are ! Perched crazily on a wooden barrow, the peasant is drawn by a lethargic horse over a stubble-field, bobbing up and down like a cork on a fishing-line. The first time I saw one of the type I could not help laughing at the odd figure bumping and dancing over the sods. Then, to saw a tree-trunk, they place it on two high trestles, lay a plank on one side, and one man above, one beneath, each with a handle of the saw, cut it into logs. A threshing-mill is worked by a horse trying to walk up a moving gangway, moved by his hoofs in their attempt to go forward. The old-time flail still serves to separate the chaff from the seed, a long pole with a shorter one hinged to it. Cows, instead of being brought into a byre, are milked outside in the fashion Hardy describes. The top bar of a gate consists of a whole tree-trunk with most of its roots attached balanced on a pole. In the smithy a handful of coke appears quite sufficient to warm a cart-wheel rim red-hot, the method being to cover the heated part with chaff, revolve the rim on a kind of stone table until the whole round is smoking. Cows, sheep, goats, and even horses are tethered and eat their circular patch.

I could write in this way for a long time, write beneath the windmill whose arms are rising and falling dizzily to a soft wind while the meal-dust flies out of the open door. The farmer is digging up his mangel-wurzels just in front of me, and a last faint gleam lies along the dark silhouette of nose and mouth.

I began the letter downcast, but now I feel quite cheerful on the subject. Nothing brings up the tone more quickly than a relieving utterance of atrabile. The air smacks fresher now, and there dwells a refreshing tang in the breeze. I feel the loss of *Forest Folk*: it reminded me of Furse's picture *Diana of the Uplands*; it had a good beginning, plenty of strong, wild colouring.

I wish I could tell where I was last month. If I come through the war, I'll be able to look on one adventure as one of the most romantic that could ever have happened to me. Coming down from the trenches, a party of three of us, dog-tired, took refuge under the tower of a great building whose name is one of the most famous of the war. There, a brilliant morning of flitting sunshine, we slept, disturbed only by the deep rumbling echoes in the superb masonry which the heaviest shell could not destroy. Among those battered ruins a lamp still swung in the close, with slender framework intact, without glass, a memory of cloistral peace. On the wall facing the street hung two gargoyles grinning with a twisted kind of animation, testifying to the living power of the man who sculptured them from the harsh stone. All the others were destroyed.

At present danger is approaching again. From now onwards I shall have need of all your hopes and desires, even prayers. That passed, I shall have some sure prospect of coming home. I found in a " Notizenbuch ", taken from a German greatcoat, the diary of one of those earnest painstaking village schoolmasters, whose work remains their pride and whole centre of life, whose ideals set a glory round their memory. It seems such a tragedy that a man like that should be forced to fight at all. But that is the tragedy for all of us.

IV

FLANDERS (*continued*)

> ZEGGERSKAPPEL,
> *10 October, 1917*

THE weather just now can be summed up in a word—wretched: not exactly wet, never dry, sometimes heavy thunder-showers, sometimes watery sunshine, placing a dead gleam on the pools and muddy roads. I have become so accustomed to "glabber" that it must be knee-deep before it disturbs me. I think it must have reached that stage in the front-line. We possess one resource, not too trustworthy duckboards: there is no fatigue more exhausting than stumbling over several miles of slippery boards with yawning shell-holes on each side, filled to the brim with foul water. The enemy usually has their range, with the result that they go up in the air every morning. Not lately, however, for his artillery has had a frightful time of it, knocked to pieces by our shells.

I expect this will be the last letter you will get from me for at least ten days. You know what that means. I can only hope to get out safely, or, at worst, with a comfortable wound. If the same fate happens to me as to Peter, I have done my duty, according to conventional standards. By higher and more ideal standards, it is too perverted to be called duty at all, if it does not immediately help to stop war and avoid sacrifice.

Our men are growing more confident every day ; in fact, one could almost go into battle now with a bag of provisions and a walking-stick. The rifle plays only a small part, for the enemy invariably throw up their hands when the infantry approach. A poor set of devils they are, too, in their barbed-wire cages ! Thin-faced, with high cheek-bones, pale as death, wearing old uniforms and cloth caps, instead of steel helmets, most of them unfeignedly glad to be well out of it, unashamed of the title of " prisoner ". The old swagger has gone out of them. Their nerves have been shaken to bits by our shells.

I found a scrap of paper with the curiously apposite verses :—

> Autour de lui, voici l'Automne à peine éclos.
> L'avalanche des fruits ruisselle, dans l'enclos,
> Le soleil chauffe et luit, le flot baisse ses rives,

FLANDERS

Et lui marche, ébloui, dans ces effluves d'or,
Accordant, prodiguant des caresses craintives
Au monde sans prise qu'il pourrait perdre encore.
" En ces jours déchirants."
HENRI DÉVIEUX.

(The warrior come home to a peaceful home-country, new to its beauty, grateful for its remembrance.)

This paper was lying beside a tombstone under the shadow of a great church. I spent an afternoon wandering round that church, sentimentalizing to my heart's content, with no one to disturb me and no one to utter bald consolations about the price of life. The slow passage of time came to a sweetness of thought, not melancholic, not poignant, just a lingering tenderness and a faint regret, tenuous as a web of sun in the tree-shadows. High chestnuts, browning through shimmering gold, dropped solitary leaves with a faint pat on the flat stones or rustled them through the wire-enclosed wreaths hanging from grey crosses, half-ruined, green with a decay of beauty, so that the harmony of life came very close to death, reality to dream. The people of this church, who lay there in the long shadow beyond the tall, iron wickerwork, were poor with an honest poverty. There was no ostentation, no flaunting sheen of marble, dead draperies, and the conventional urns, but a misty angel in a corner, with bowed head, like melancholy smiling with a vague sweetness of grief, as if all the rudeness and directness of earth had melted away to pale beauty in those tenderly clasped hands, and human sorrow become radiant glory, shrined in peaceful acquiescence. Nowhere could one escape, or did wish to escape, that haunting thought of death glorified to the angel, decay become a slumbering beauty beneath those slowly-heaving chestnut branches with their constant murmur of dropping leaves touched to earth by a gentle wind. The church had buttresses at equal distance, and between them, half-obscured, vaguely splendid still were paintings of Christ and the Virgin, the Father throned in a chalky glory, and angels with flaking wings flying to a cornice where swallows were twittering and hovering, silent as ghosts, with spots of silver on their wings as they swooped into the sun and came back again to shadow. Before the arched entrance were two statues—two saints probably—rudely sculptured, with falling features so that the noses were mere blotches and the ears had been rubbed close to the head. Outside, on the square, there lay a broad, golden sunshine, so peaceful, so mellow, so radiant, that it seemed war had lapsed into mystery and all the agonies of life smoothed down to a haunting dream.

You will see the old sentiments cannot die, and it is not desirable they should. They are worth something more than this, see farther and higher, and have a longer value. Not ephemeral, but progressive and continuous on a way of perfection.

.   .   .   .   .

(Written in Hospital.)

Le Treport,
12 October, 1917

I got that comfortable wound I mentioned in my last letter: some intuition must have told me what was going to happen. The pain is not too great, although the right leg is useless just now; the doctor says it will come in time. I am expecting to be home in two days. As soon as he heard of the division to which I belonged, then it was all right: the fighting divisions, if they don't get much of a time in the trenches, are decently treated in hospital, have usually the precedence, and rightly, too.

I just want to tell you about the last affair.

Our division had the pleasing task of making a bold bid for Passchendaele : of course, the officers told us the usual tale, " a soft job ", and I reckon it might have been easy enough if we had had a decent start. But none of us knew where to go when the barrage began, whether half-right or half-left : a vague memory of following the shell-bursts as long as the smoke was black, and halting when it changed to white. It was all the same to me : I was knocked out before I left the first objective, a ghastly breast-work littered with German corpses. One sight almost sickened me before I went on : thinking the position of a helmet on a dead officer's face rather curious, sunken down rather far on the nose, my platoon sergeant lifted it off, only to discover no upper half to the head. All above the nose had been blown to atoms, a mass of pulp, brain, bone and muscle.

Apart from that, the whole affair appeared rather good fun. You know how excited one becomes in the midst of great danger. I forgot absolutely that shells were meant to kill and not to provide elaborate lighting effects, looked at the barrage, ours and the German's, as something provided for our entertainment—a mood of madness, if you like. The sergeant's face struck me most, grey and drawn, blanched as if he had just undergone a deadly sickness. There was death in it, if ever death can be glimpsed in the living. A fat builder, loaded with five hundred rounds, acted the brave man, ran on ahead, signalled back to us, and in general acted as if on a quiet parade. The last I saw of him was two arms straining madly at the ground, blood pouring from his mouth, while legs and body sunk into a shell-hole filled with water. One Highlander, raving mad, shouted to us, " Get on, you cowards, why don't you run at them ? " As if running could be contemplated with a barrage going twenty-five yards a minute.

Then the enemy put up a counter-barrage, something to make the hair stand on end, shells tripping over each other, gas sending out a horrible smell of mustard, shrapnel whirring just over our heads, and a strange explosive which ran along the ground in yellow flame for yards and took the feet from us. We rested in a shell-hole for a minute, just to give our nerves a rest and escape the machine-gun bullets which pattered thickly on the ground all round us. I saw one gentleman going through the pockets of a dead German, very careful to unpin the Iron Cross colours on the breast. May he have good luck for his thieving!

The lighting effect appeared in great glory, superb in a word. The enemy knew exactly when the barrage would begin, for at 5.30 he sent up long streamers of green stars and a strange arabesque of yellow, red, and crimson lights; Vèry lights hovered all over the sky already paling in a grey bleak dawn. Then with a continuous drumming our shells burst on him; before us the country seemed a mass of crawling flame, wave after wave of it, until the clouds were blotted out, and our men advancing into it grew nightmarish, as if under a cliff of fire. Vaguely, in the distance, several dark forms could be seen running over a ridge, the enemy retiring to be out of range. I had seen a dark blotch to the right, and was going towards it, thinking it a machine-gun post in our advanced line, when the enemy counter-barrage surrounded it and spread in long lines behind us. Thus we were shut in, and the only thing to do was to advance. Some of our shells fell short and exploded in isolated groups of men. But when the mud and smoke cleared away, there they were, dirty but untouched. The clay, rain-soaked, sucked in the shell and the shrapnel seemed to get smothered, making it useless. One from the enemy fell behind me and made me gasp as if some one had poured cold water down the back. A man beside me put his hands to his ears with a cry of horror, stone-deaf, with ear-drums shattered.

We got the first objective easily, and I was leaning against the side of a shell-hole, resting along with some others, when an aeroplane swooped down and treated us to a shower of bullets. None of them hit. I never enjoyed anything so much in my life—flames, smoke, lights, S.O.S.s, drumming of guns, and swishing of bullets, appeared stage-properties to set off a great scene. From the pictorial point of view nothing could be finer or more majestic; it had a unity of colour and composition all its own, the most delicate shades of green and grey and brown fused wonderfully in the opening light of morning. When the barrage lifted and the distant ridge gleamed dark against the horizon, tree-stumps, pill-boxes, shell-holes, mine-craters, trenches, shone but faintly, fragmentary in the drifting smoke. Dotted here and there, in their ghostly helmets and uniforms, the enemy were hurrying off or coming down in batches to find their own way to the cages. They knew our lines better than we. Nothing fulfils the childish idea of a ghoul more satisfactorily than those prisoners, mud-befouled, unshaven, terror-stricken, tattered, and heavily booted, with their huge helmets protecting the head so closely.

Then, going across a machine-gun barrage, I got wounded. At first I did not know where, the pain was all over, and then the gushing blood told me. The problem now lay in front, how to get through the double barrage of machine-guns and shells the enemy had put behind our advancing columns. I decided to make a run for it, but knew not where to run, and followed a German prisoner to an advanced dressing-station, where four men carried me on a stretcher down the Passchendaele road, over a wilderness of foul holes littered with dead men disinterred in the barrage. One sight I remember very vividly: a white-faced German prisoner tending a whiter " Cameron " who had been struck in the stomach. In spite of the fierce shell-fire he did not leave him, but stayed by him as long as I could see. I confess my first feeling of deadly fear arose when on the stretcher. The first excitement was wearing off and my teeth were shattering with cold. Besides, shrapnel was drumming overhead, along the line of the duckboard track. Nothing frightens one more than high shrapnel, a blow from it is almost certain death, for the bullets strike the head first and there remains no way of escaping. With a high-explosive one can side-slip or lie down beside it, letting the stuff go over. An old soldier can tell to a nicety where a shell will land, and makes off to suit, but high shrapnel bursts around one before the hearing or even instinct can warn. I saw two men carrying a wounded Highlander killed at the same time, while the latter got off scot-free; the only trouble was his being dropped into a stinking shell-hole. I came down myself once or twice, the path being so bad, but my stretcher bearers, R.A.M.C., were good stuff, afraid of nothing, and kind-hearted, apologizing for any jolting. How they kept it up during that ghastly 10-kilometre journey is a mystery. I would rather go over the top than suffer that fatigue.

LE TREPORT,
16 October, 1917

Being in bed all day with nothing to do, I might describe that wonderful canal-bank at Ypres I mentioned some time ago, and also our march to Passchendaele, thus finishing the whole matter at once when memory is fresh. That march from Vlamertinghe to Ypres at night must remain the most romantic and exciting incident of my life, not on account of bursting shells or even danger in its slightest form, but through the uncertain nature of our road, and the warnings we received as to spies. My duty was to link up companies, our company being behind " C ". Whenever the men in front diverged from the straight track, I had to wait behind and tell the following which way they had taken. With the night pitch-black and a bewildering procession of G.S. wagons, transport, guns, and ammunition-carts all over the landscape, such a procedure was by no means a joke. If the company got lost through me, there would be a hot time in store : no reward, of course, if I was successful.

At sunset the battalion set out, each company with its set of pipers and drummers. The sky, from being a wonderful mauve-purple of great brilliancy where white balloons hung ghostlike and smoke from distant shells hovered mysteriously dim, grew dark almost at once ; trees crept back into shadow, and the road, from a golden continuity, sunk into nothing. No outline lay on anything—ruins, hedges, fields, ditches, disappearing in an intense darkness. Then my troubles began. First of all, my company got muddled up behind two wagons, each of which had fallen into the ditch on either side of the road. The distance between the two companies grew alarmingly great, and I had almost despaired when the confusion ceased and all was right again. Then I spent some time telling an over-inquisitive officer my duties did not lie in telling which battalion I belonged to and where it was going, that he had better wait until the Adjutant arrived, and ask him. We had been warned so earnestly about spies, and that this attack of the division must remain absolutely unknown even to our own army that I was afraid to say a word. When I left him and hurried on, I plumped into a cross-roads with no sign of any one to direct us anywhere : at random I asked an artilleryman where the company in front had gone, and with relief learned the road. There, two hundred yards farther, I found it halted behind a lumbering wagon. The difficulty now lay in keeping the companies apart.

That difficulty surmounted, off we went again. An engineer walked along with me for some distance and at the last gave me a packet of biscuits, with the cry of " Cheery-o, good luck on Thursday ". He belonged to our division and knew when the attack was coming off. I never felt so glad in all my life when our Quartermaster hailed me and took over duty as guide. Then, stumbling down a rutty road lined with trees, lights glinting at intervals, we came to a bridge over a dull-gleaming water, and got into dug-outs for the night.

. . . . .

(Written in the train going to Le Havre.)

18 October, 1917

The most poignant recollection of the canal bank lies in a picture I saw early in the morning of the next day. After stumbling up a stair of planks, we got on the left bank itself and dropped into a deep trench that seemed to twist about in a most tantalizing fashion. At last we struck a low passage and came to rest in a chamber abutting on it, made of heavy corrugated-iron bent over to touch the ground on each side. Within this space hung four wire-beds fastened with string : I got into the frailest, and no one can quite imagine the miserable time I had all night wondering when I would drop on the man beneath as one strand parted after another.

In a grey dawn I decided to explore a little farther, and went down the passage, still half-asleep and shivering with cold. A track of light to the left showed where the entrance lay, and I was going joyfully towards it when a strange figure, silhouetted in the opening, made me sick and sent me hurriedly back to where I came. It was a man astride across the light, fallen on his face with both legs projecting. He had been there for years, for the skin stretched black over sharp bones, and the tunic, faded with weather, showed blood-stains like blotches on old parchment. In terror he had essayed to escape a shell, but the shell had got him first. I have seen some dreadful sights, but none penetrated so deeply as that. Remember it was early morn, the time when the body and mind are more open to impression, more easily affected by the unforeseen, and that I had spent a sleepless night fighting against straining nerves. The sight of that poor fellow sent a shrinking into my very soul; heart, blood, flesh, all the generous vitalities were shrivelled up, and a vague, wild, barren terror took their place. I could not think: the ostrich instinct was on me and I would gladly have hidden anywhere to escape it.

That quality of horror pervades the canal bank: there must have been dreadful fighting there at one time, for both sides of the canal, high banks just raised like mounds above the surrounding country, are still strewn with men dead years ago and burnt up like mummies by the weather. On the enemy side of the bank stretch miles of water-logged shell-holes and craters, where men lie thickly, obscene masses of decay, shapeless and distorted, some bunched up, others with legs or arms rising blackly above the mud, others buried to the head with horrible faces on a level with the ground. The atmosphere dwells heavy, and a slight but penetrating smell of decay spreads over everything; the water of the canal itself rolls along sluggishly as if weighted with blood. The reeds cluster more rankly and thickly, the grass twists more intricately, and nature has a strong growth, unhealthy in rottenness. In the distance rise the tower and spire of Ypres as peaceful in the purple shimmer as a village at home: not a shell bursts anywhere for a moment; the clouds rest in misty flocks on the ridge, and in finely graded perspective, the grey and green monotony of shell-holes disappears into the full-bosomed sky. Even Belgium has its beauty, and the spirit, dwelling only on it, lays aside all thought of death, content to rest awhile in vision.

I was perched on the bank beneath a gaunt tree, thinking of nothing at all, only trying to find points of comparison between Morris's description of the " Dry Tree " in the *Well at the World's End* ", and this in front of me, when Johnson asked me to look at the afterglow effect on a row of tall trees reflected in the water. The sky gleamed and glinted living gold, and the canal repeated its glory, touching it softly in the shadow with azure : against them the gaunt, leafless trees told startlingly, pure black against the flaming colour tossed from distant ridge to ridge and their reflections interrupted by long bars of cool twilight held in water, stretched darkly and mysteriously to the tall reeds where a bare-chested artilleryman was washing shirt and tunic. I had never looked at this corner before : I was so busy looking towards Ypres. But of all the perfect Corotesque pictures I have glimpsed in France, this one transcended all. There dwelt a haunting majesty about it as if it were built on dreams and might fade away at a touch. Nothing substantial, yet nothing tenuous, the fine material for a glorious conception. After all, it was worth while, even in Belgium, to have spent a minute before such a strange beauty, to have fatigue crowned a moment of such glory. Every one who has seen that row of trees must have felt like that. I did, at any rate, and my companion. The only image I could satisfy my mood in reference to this beauty and horror of the canal bank was of a gaily-painted snake whose bite was poison.

(On board the Hospital Ship.)

19 October, 1917

You will remember the strong, hard faces, held in the unnatural light Brangwyn paints occasionally : that memory realized remains one of the most poignant of my experience. The night previous to the attack we lined up along the canal bank, and as I peered into each face to find my section, the harsh unnatural look was in all, that strange repellent tenseness of feature and expression caused by intense emotion—emotion not only of nerves strung to the utmost pitch, but of body, for almost every man had a dose of rum. The platoon officer, usually a quiet retiring lad, not over-confident, surprised me with a mouthful of curses for being late. It might appear bravado, but I think I was the only cool one among them, actuated by a sense of wonder at so much excitement. After all, the business had to be done, and there was no use burking it or flying into hysterics. The lucky, chosen men would come back, the others would not. That appeared the sum total, in my modest judgment. Perhaps lack of rum caused this apparent indifference. From the working of his features I thought the officer drunk, but from then until the time I was wounded I lost sight of him.

Then the rifle grenadiers—I was one—slipped on their makeshift bags of bombs, bags made of sandbag with bands of split puttee. If there is an agony comparable to that strain on the shoulder caused by a dangling weight of a dozen grenades, when the pins and rods project and dig into the ribs at every step, I would accept it with wonder as being something unearthly. Then the beastly puttee-band broke in two and I had to fasten it round a corner of the bag. I have lost count of the times that band was fastened. At every jolt it would drop with a thud, and at every irregularity the whole weight would shift forward and bow me down like an old cab-horse unable to see the ground. With a groan I would pitch the ghastly thing back and then the band flew loose. Thus the rotten game started again. The man in front was palpably nervous; he lost trace of his forerunners time and again, and the whole company would stop till he made good. Every hole in the duckboard track seemed to put the fear of death in him, for he spent valuable minutes gingerly picking his steps, while the men behind me cursed and swore. At last I drew my bayonet and told him the next time he stopped he would stop on its point. That cured him; he didn't lose connection again.

The dramatic entered into the business. After going about eight kilometres, across a road where a transport lay shattered with men and mules scattered about, the work of a shell not ten minutes before, we entered the salient. Then no one could have told from what direction the shells were coming; they whistled and screamed behind, before, beside, until one thought the air so full of them that the mere matter of putting up a hand would be a sure way of encountering one at least. We passed a crowd of ambulance men carrying away wounded men who had been lying out for days. The shells began to burst very close; one dud almost hit me on the toes. That incident decided me: it was bad enough facing shells without courting destruction by carrying bombs. With that, too, the man in front turned round and asked me, "When are you dropping the bombs?" "Oh! wait another hundred yards!" After going about twenty, he asked again. "Good God! When are you dropping the bombs?" Just then a shell-hole answered him, for in falling into it the whole affair slipped into the water, and I arose a lighter man. "Oh! drop them now", I whispered, and the four of them got rid of the nuisance furtively without a sound of splash as the bags disappeared into the slimy pools.

Then rain came down, the true Belgian blend. Like the others, I carried a spade between the pack and back. I never knew how thoroughly soaked one can be in a few minutes on account of this arrangement. The spade-shank led the water nicely to the very small of the back. In a trice a river was running inside my trousers and over every part of the body. A strong wind blew, and the feeling of cold was so intensified that the bravest of us longed for a shell to come and end our misery. We stood for six hours in that blinding rainstorm, in battle position, before the order came to get into shell-holes. This was no easy matter, for every hole appeared a veritable quagmire, where one sunk to the knees in glutinous mud. I found a fairly dry one, and had just scooped out a nice comfortable recess where I could shelter from the wind when the barrage began.

Then, with rifles slung, and great trepidation in our hearts, we scrambled up, in any formation at all, and went forward into the heart of the flame.

ZEGGERSKAPPEL,
October 1917

The stoic doctrine remains the only pillar of faith that can support the soldier, not by the skill of his arm or his strength, but by undoubting trust in good luck and sure Fate is he able to withstand a deadly sickness of disillusionment and horror of disaster.

If I had a confidence that the war would soon finish, I could think myself in Elysium, an Elysium of peaceful beauty. Association enters, for the park where we are resting has all the quiet elements which go to form the subdued landscape beloved of the moderns: a profusion of twisted, grey fruit trees rising over a grassy elevation to gleam pale against a fringe of woodland; red-tiled farm-buildings on a structure of rough beams and yellowish clay mellowed by atmosphere to a fine series of warm-purple tints; a broad-hatted peasant turning the handle of a draw-well; brown cows grazing in the middle distance, with legs hidden below the grass-tops; and an infinity of butterflies rising and falling among the flowers. When we wake in the morning, the peacefulness of the whole glides like a dream into the perception, and the contrast grows the more bitter till we wonder why we are living at all.

The men here think me wonderfully religious, especially when I told them I was reading the Bible in the guise of Dante's *Inferno*. He hits the present state of affairs very nicely :—

> Virtù così per nemica si fuga
> Da tutte, come biscia, o per ventura
> Del loco o per mal uso chè li fruga.

I think the Gaderene swine led a preferable existence to ours; they incurred a more comfortable death. When an army goes

into the trenches, with the resigned despair
of an Oriental going to torture, " Kismet "
on the lips, then there is little hope of real
enthusiastic action, or even attempt at action.
The war has given birth to that weird courage
which inspires a man to great bravery even
when he knows no reward will or can possibly
accrue : the daring is reasoned, like the
clarity of a man meeting death open-eyed
and never wavering, even an eye-lid. I can
see it in the men around me—men who have
been wounded and gone home, who possess
no illusions about its horror, yet go willingly
enough without cowardly shrinking or backward appeal. I have always that fear beside
me, the fear of showing myself unworthy,
cowardly—if I had that mastered, or even
shelved, I could be as resigned as the others ;
but the future haunts one so much—the
war has deepened, I think, and vivified my
sensations of everything. Imagination draws
up a plan of free development of faculty
if this present obstacle were surmounted ;
but, in surmounting, the ditch lies waiting,
and not a few fall into it, never to rise again,
or at best maimed. The fortunate topple
over to the other side with the nightmare
ever present.

WINIZEELE,
October **1917**

I cannot state even now with clear detail what happened to me in the trenches last week. There is still a confusion in me and around me so that I cannot define clearly the clouds hovering in the limpid sky or the dark trees by the way. You know that strange exalted feeling that comes after a confrontation with unexpected soul-stirring beauty. It might be possible to make a strange etherealized religion from **the horrors** of the life and the landscape of green, slimy shell-holes, where legs project and arms lie floating on rottenness, a new, old belief in beauty harmonized in suffering, of calm sky drawn down yearningly to an instinctive mood, of subtle glories taken from abhorrence, frail shadowy life from hideous death. I think and think of that new religion until the will surrenders to the yearning and the vision grows dim, blurring harsh outline and softening raw colour to a pale radiance containing all the glory and slowly palpitating joy of earth; I think bitterness could not be more intense, or disgust more keen, until this strange reconciliation creeps softly to the mood, and, like a trembling sunlight on the hills, flashes and gleams in wistful loveliness. I look down into myself, a boundless thing where there is no end and no fathomable inspiration, an invisible world of dream, where the memory cherishes the faint, pure beauties of the life, distills them to a haunting grace, and thrusts out with repulsion all that smacks of sordid horrors and sensuous delight. A fine voluptuary of earthly delights, yet a seeker of a lost hope vaguely shadowed beyond earth, and only attainable in a future infinitely remote. Thought, once inspired, takes up those frail threads one by one and tries to weave from them a garment, but where the subtle vision tires or rests they fall asunder and the clear world emerges, bereft of glory and naked of soul-beauty, a harsh ignoble thing, rawly splendid. Yet I think a race will come after us who will make that beauty a real thing, evolve a religion more noble than the conventional trust in God, thrust aside superstition, narrow individualism, narrow nationalism, and all the peoples of earth, filled with a new yearning, come together to banish ugliness and join together in the realization of this beauty.

Even now, when a great yellow band lies immobile between dark sky and darker land, when a group of soldiers passing over a duckboard track stands silhouetted against it and delicate lines of fire outline their shadow, I have a vague perception of a harmony which will come, even as vaguely silhouetted against the years, even as vaguely ennobled in the fire of sacrifice, even as statuesque in the silvery glories of the sky. Sometimes that passion grows so intense that the spirit seems to crumble away and the whole of life is full of an intolerable yearning. I stretch hands to the stars, and when they sink listlessly to the ground, the roar of a gun breaks the silence, and against the horizon trembles and flashes a Very light or the yellow radiance of a fire. Then the memory grows dull and the vision dead, until the thought comes that all endeavour is useless, all aspirations foolish, all yearning purposeless, and forgetfulness the end of all. Sadness and a wistful melancholy creep in ; one loses touch of the world and half hopes that oblivion and death would come ; but the spirit pulses on, and the white clouds sailing grandly to a shadowy horizon appear great wings from earth to heaven, the human will a slumbering recognition of the divine. Dream glorifies ; the spirit, chastened, thrills to the subtle music, and beauty comes, in trembling radiance, to kiss the soul to life.

GLASGOW,
11 November, 1917

Perhaps when the matter remains by me I might resume my ideas concerning the Passchendaele Ridge battle, not the historic, but the purely individual—something of the soul and nothing of the material. What can be the value of any thought expressed as a form of literature, even in embryo as it is in my letters, when it deals with mere ephemeral attributes, things passing, even now past and gone to a limbo unregretted perhaps, vague monuments to perverted endeavour ? I can still see those guns ranged along the Menin Road; their heads crowned with laurel leaves, which, on nearer approach, were bits of green paper strung on nets. A curious association, that of the laurel leaf : Ariosto and Tasso were crowned with it to express a love of serene, sun-flooded beauty ; now we crown them to express our admiration of nature, not beautiful, but strictly utilitarian. Old Silenus rarified to a Bacchic diety, and then degraded to a brutal licence of destruction ; his grapes, drops of vivid blood ! That is the only image

I can picture when I see those fat-bellied monsters coughing flame. Grant us, then, the image—what lives ?—is it the image or the gun ? Will we not condemn the gun as the symbol of sheer horror, nightmarish, drowning the fine sparks of the nobly beautiful showered on the soul from the eternal. We have those sparks, every one, the frail immortal glory hovering, vaguely incandescent, with a firm sheath of flesh : every one, even the drunkard vomiting over a bridge with vacant eye and an ever-flowing curse, has that tenuous beauty which will spread forth until the gorgeous wonder of its origin is disclosed and we know the eternal.

Not licentiousness, not debauchery, not extravagance, not voluptuousness, not bestiality can touch it, for they are sins of the flesh—surface sins. The sin of war is not surface ; it goes to the very heart and centre of being, for the thought is ever poised of life dormant given to death—death a present thing, waiting eagerly behind the beauty of the day, coming forward in the mystery of night. This reflection destroys every longing for the unattainable, for the glory, for the radiant unknown, and centres on the body itself, a grovelling physical fear rarefied and intensified to spiritual debasement. The gun symbolizes all that hideous degradation, that smurring of the fine soul.

The image then, what is it? Is it not an attempt to ennoble this spiritual debasement, this clouding of the soul by weaving fantastic colour round the symbol? Perhaps, if one thinks this vision-stealing implies concurrence. To me it represents an attempt to escape from the sordid reality into that gracious world of beauty we left behind us when we donned armour and shouldered packs. It is the effort to recapture that immaterial delight of long ago, the psychological expression of a poignant longing grown to an intensity of agony unknown and impossible before. It would be difficult to find anguish quite so bitter as that futile endeavour of the soul thirsting for beauty to conciliate with and fuse into the preconceived ideal of beauty, the hideous aspect, the base phenomena of modern war.

But the question arises—might we not create a new ideal which will really get behind, not only the ancient longings, but also the present horrors; get to a more fundamental ideal than all those enumerated, an ideal which will explain everything in terms of beauty and inspire with the divine? Many a time I have tried that, and failed, content only with partial glimpses, swift glintings of light on a bosom as the goddess fades, frail gleams tenuous as the grey light touched to glory in a clear dawn. But the effort was there and compensated for eternal misery with a self-forgetfulness, a sinking into oblivion of dream.

I remember one memorable day I spent in the square at St. Pol, a brilliant day of sun with great clouds quiescent in infinite purple. I noted the impressions of that rapture of soul opening to sky and golden earth :—

"There remains still a vague bitterness as if one could not seize all the floating impressions of life in the air and, dissatisfied, took refuge in self, dimly aware of cowardice, and yet conscient of failure in the intuition to grasp that impalpable influence shown in so many wonderful things, 'effluves de la beauté', which come round the eyes and blind them to all but an intense irradiation flooding down from the immensity of sky. The great clouds in a limpid sea, purely white with suave purple shadows, lose their haunting power to instil a desire for rest under a bounteous sun; they are barriers to that power which lies behind them and sprays through them, coming to rest on the broad yellow gleam before me, tremulous in the indistinct shadow of sun diluted and thinly washed over masonry, a fretted cornice, a bowed Atlas supporting an arch. The vision grasps alone the eternal purport of that gleam; men and women lose shadow and form in it; the world is but a finely limned ecstasy of light—radiant, serene, grandly beautiful; the body droops away, and the eyes sees but a shivering haze in a golden beauty; the senses blur but to that gracious light, and the longings, the passions, the exquisite griefs of the heart vanish: no sweetness could be more poignant, no happiness so delicately wonderful as that lingering in gleam, the slow drowning in an infinite sea."

Words, words, immaterial words, you might say, and liken them to froth in a glass, full of light and colour, but empty, meaningless, useless: perhaps—but they mean something very definite to me; they are not words alone, but symbols, the utterance of an immaterial ecstasy of feeling only to be expressed in gossamer, the imponderable glory of surrender to inseizable influence, emanation from earth luminous in a dawn of perception.

That attempt to answer intuitively the call of the beautiful in nature, even in the bleak horror of shell-holes, seemed the essence of life to me, the only thing worth seeking in the misery of this war. The call was everywhere, a fascinating thing ; even within the fetid, slimy horror, of shell-holes it vibrated, for even there beauty smurred the filth with pure green and brought grass over it to hide the wound. But the final beauty of all lay in the spirit itself, its change, its exaltations and ecstasies, its depressions and griefs, despair and madness ; the infinite was touching it to life, and its movements were part of the infinite itself.

A glorification of spirit undoubtedly, but if one neglected this spirit and faced reality, then life would have been unbearable in its bleak misery : cowardice, yet justifiable cowardice, for there are other things in life than transfixing an enemy with the bayonet. There were no gleams on anything beyond what the mind or vision huddled to itself of reflected beauty expanding to the outer world, and laying colour on it : the mind placed its own gleams, and thought grew acquiescent, content to dwell in oblivion. The visionary triumphed over the warrior, and war itself became an abstraction, known only to a nightmarish imagination.

. . . . .

The only thing our so-called admirers at home praised in the Passchendaele campaign was the heroism of the soldier; they might go a little further now and curse those men who led us into this ghastly shambles. What use was it for us to add a little more flesh and bone to that sewage-heap! What conceivable value could such surrender of clean, good life be to the glory of a country eulogized by paunchy carpet-knights! The Passchendaele battle had absolutely nothing to recommend it—military, strategic, political, moral: every one felt when he was picking a gluey way over noisome shell-holes, beside poor broken relics of humanity, among bursting shells, that he was picking a way to death, certainly not to a glory of victory. The dull ache kept us in that silent misery which cannot be relieved by curses: with it was the feeling that we were paying rather dearly for this firework pageant, not so much with life as with self-respect. Don Quixotes resuscitated, tilting at windmills with as little purpose! With his illusion all might have sounded glorious, romantic; we might have been fraying wings in an immense effort to get to the beyond, the cynosure of the world, the mailed incarnation of heroism dauntless to death, carving the world with a superb disdain, a frenzy of fine gesture.

The theatrical properties had disappeared, however—Columbine degenerated to a frowsy Fleming dispensing miserable coffee, Harlequin a naked wretch with not a spangle on him, not a single sequin to clothe his frail humanity. We were just Pulcinellos without the lustre, fools doing foolish things, and unable to do otherwise under force of compulsion. If we looked back we were shot; if we went forward we had a clear possibility of death. The most sanguine of us could quite well, like Maître François, betray a very intimate knowledge of death: not a "Ballade des Pendus", but a "Sheep's Saunter into Hell".

There was no morale in the Flanders offensive, no infective enthusiasm, for even to tilt at windmills, the mind must have something definite before it, some real purpose: but the Flanders offensive was a ghastly mistake, and we knew it. Without incentive, what could be expected. We are united in our devotion to impulse, and when the impulse is not there, then we become shadows of men, aimless spectres chasing vainly a gleam, striving to be contented with the froth instead of drinking the rich wine in long heady draughts.

Our friends at home expanded chests at the thought of heroism at Passchendaele; but was it heroism that should ever have been demanded from the Army? Was it not rather a disgraceful trifling with the most sacred instincts of life, when the soldier was asked to perform deeds of bleak horror unrelieved by purpose or even success? Now that the business is over, the soldier cannot look back on shell-holes and acres of dead Germans as monuments to the heroism of the British Army: he has a dim sense of shame as at some unnatural, disgraceful thing he was forced to do, which neither instinct, sentiment, nor reason could invest with pride. With that comes the ironic feeling of sacrifice to the political intrigues of worthless statesmen: we could not explain the Passchendaele offensive from a military point of view, consequently we could only see in it a political, a calm, cold-blooded sacrifice of life for miserable diplomatic advancement. The only image of it that came to the mind was that of a man patting familiarly on the back, but in reality seeking the right place to sink the knife. We were bespattered with words of praise from Army commanders, from Jingo newspapers, were termed Sir Galahads whetting a lance in the battle of chivalry. When I read the Prime Minister's glorification of Britain as an altruistic, disinterested hero fighting the fight of freedom, I could only think—was there ever such a barefaced perversion of truth expressed by a statesman before, or was the man totally mad and actually believed it? Besides, Sir Galahad, in the modern estimate, was only a fool, doing foolish things, and to liken us to him, appeared the reverse of complimentary, either to Sir Galahad or us. Sir Galahad did fight clean if he mistook his target, whereas we, with our stinking gas and drumming shells, fought against Nature herself, against the primal dictates of humanity. Our explosives smashed humanity into obscene fragments of blood and dirt, disinterred old, putrid bodies, made a frightful shipwreck of the finer feelings, and changed every one into a blind brute mouthing words of hatred, swallowing curses down the throat to poison the whole spiritual purity of heart and soul.

Just now, when I can see the sky through an open window—for the day has been golden with mellow sun—I think life is a very beautiful thing, a quiet sufficiency of happiness culled from the sky and earth, a noble suffusion of gleam, God's breath dimly luminous on the soul like a glass. The sky shines in a wonderful gradation of pale mauve to rose-pink, very delicate as if it were too tenuous even to shimmer in the depths, a ghost of colour; clouds raise sleepy heads with golden edges of flame where the afterglow has rested on them, and at the roof of a grey building a heavy boulder is lying, sullenly, as if to roll over the slates and drop in snow on my bed. Then, as I watch, delicately, softly, purely, like a touch of mystery shedding colour on a dream, a grey veil comes over so slowly that the eye cannot keep pace with it, but races forward; the clouds sink in it like down, and soon a great hand of pale purple stretches over the sky as if to bless the world with a hope of cloistral peace. It seems almost a presence sent expressly to cheer; the spirit willingly loses touch of earth; nurses, men in blue, doctors, white beds, striated pillars, brown floors, everything disappears, and I am alone in the world, alone with that infinite sea lined by a window; the sense of vastness enters into perception; the heart loses a beat; there is a choking sensation in the throat; hands are thrust out blindly to ward off a blow, and I am lying, stricken, back on a pillow, striving to see the white roof overhead, and bewildered by a flashing myriad of stars, flickering and pointing. There is nothing real : under the eyelids, a flickering green shot with gold and black ; the eyes open to darkness and memory is quiescent, spirit dead but to that mystery of cloud and sky. Then reality comes back with a jerk : I am sitting up once more in bed, admiring in a vague way a lonely square of golden light resting on the counterpane, while a blur of blue and grey tells me a nurse has just passed into the next ward.

There are other glories in life than a senseless rushing over No Man's Land into an improbable victory : glory is a silent thing, a chaste thing sent from a great beneficent power to ennoble the spirit ; it lives in the air, in the walls, in the pillars, in the beds, and comes through them to perception and thence to a wondering adoration ennobled by obedience. Silence and a slow tasting, drop by drop, deliciously and delicately until the soul is sated and there grieves nothing ; restless ambition sinks into acquiescence, and the whole of life becomes rarefied, body essentialized, spirit given broad wings to bear it through the ether ; the world becomes a seal and symbol of an everlasting communion, heart taken into the great heart, soul into the great soul. That perception of self governed by self is the supreme value war has had for me; it forced me back on myself and on my comrades, inspired with desire to get something better and more eternal out of life than physical enjoyment.

I read a book by Moselly, *L'Aube fraternelle*, which recalls strangely my own idealistic tendencies. The hero has written his experiences of military life in France during peace, with much the same insistence on the psychological expression as I. After a trying day, he takes rest in a "cabaret" and abandons himself to the delicious feeling of rest :—

Puis ces détails même m'échappent, et je sombre doucement dans une torpeur délicieuse, où je m'abandonne sans cesse au charme consolant du présent et à sa tiédeur. Plus de pensée nette, d'inquiétude d'avenir, de regrets, d'âme. Il me semble que les impressions du dehors pénètrent en moi, s'y installent, y mettent de l'ordre et du calme et renvoient en moi ancien, inquiet, et tourmenté. Mon âmi est pleine d'une joie abondante et confuse, d'une sensation inexprimable de bien-être, qui s'étale en moi, comme de larges flots, où surnagent seulement quelques perceptions éclatantes, qui me rendent plus heureux, sans que j'en aie bien conscience : la couleur rouge vif des géraniums posés sur le rebord de la fenêtre, l'eau qui tombe sur la place voisine, dans la fontaine, le bruit mat d'une boule qui roule sur la terre, dans le jeu de quilles, sous les arbres du jardin.

That is my philosophy of life exactly: the spirit distills the world to spirit; the harsh, brutal, horrible, material things to beauty; the most fugitive sensations to expression and recognition of the eternal. The whole function of life is to gather together all those different things into one, into the eternal purpose, into the eternal beauty, become conscient and palpitating through the world. With that thought life anywhere should be bearable even in the rotting horrors of Flanders: actual existence, actual suffering, does not matter in this recognition of the divine clothed in beauty. The business of life is to silhouette every manifestation, animate or inanimate, against a sky of perception so that the vague gleam in everything may be displayed and its light be added to that within. Fatalism undoubtedly, but a noble Fatalism! Epicureanism, but a very exquisite Epicureanism! Pantheism, but a very individual Pantheism! Deism, but a restricted form of Deism, the recognition of beauty as being the prime motive of the universe! My ideal remains, after all, the old classic ideal, glorified by Carducci and yet humbled by him to a somewhat meretricious Christianity, adoration of a symbol. We must build up our own religion, our own ideal. What was good enough for our grandfathers is not good enough for us. There is nothing in creation good enough for us. We are the only good thing in creation. Perhaps excessive egoism, perhaps too sweeping a gesture! But we must have courage and confidence to follow the gleam, whatever it is; and if those dead things we call tradition and time hang on our heels, then let us cut them off and race forward to the dawn. If the individual can ennoble his conception of life by his conception of the eternal beauty, there will be no need for ranting psalm-singers or slushy sermonists, but a grateful, humble acquiescence in the Divine, an ever-dauntless effort to reach the ideal, to find full happiness in life itself and not in a cowardly trust in immortality—golden wings after death.

In the bed opposite mine there is the only hero I have ever met. He had been wounded over a year ago by shrapnel in the right thigh. While he was lying on the field, a German came up and transfixed him through the lower part of the stomach. Thus with two almost mortal wounds, this poor fellow was taken to hospital and fought for life a whole year in France. Even in this hospital he has undergone three operations; his right leg has been severed, and for weeks his life hung by a thread. Yet just now he is laughing at a comrade across the passage, crying out jokes to him as if nothing in the world was wrong; always cheerful, except when pain makes him wince, he symbolizes the very noblest type of manhood I have ever seen, or shall ever see. I don't think anything would be too good for him. He remains infinitely superior to myself: if I had had those wounds, I should have given up the ghost long ago—and surrendered in sheer despair.

War has ennobled the man to the angel, has stamped in gold the finest part of him, yet at what a price, what an agony, what a desecration of life! With that note of horror I shall close, for if every one could visualize always this horror and know its human application, war would absolutely cease, and our ruddy generals find a new occupation other than that of spreading an aureole round hell. There is only one thing real in life, and that is eternity. War remains at best a nauseous blasphemy.

A DEATH IN HOSPITAL

At evening, when the night was dark outside,
And noise of children playing came in through the windows;
Voices in chorus haltingly, a ring of passing feet,
A distant blare of bands, a faint, faint tinkle of pianos,
And suddenly the lovely tolling of a single bell!

Dear Heart, how longingly, I thought of thee,
When nurses tip-toed round that bed, red-eyed,
And stole away to hide their sobbing in the corridors,
Afraid that even that pale face should stir to sound,
Wrapped in the last great calm that only is angelic—
Then from the bed, a rasp of breath in long intake and shuddering fall!

A DEATH IN HOSPITAL

We held our hearts, we who had life to live,
And thought our thoughts, but said nothing
Of that deep fear which stirs the soul of man
When brothers go from them and give from dust
A new-won soul within the hand of God.

Then, at the close a whisper—that was all—
We knew that one brave heart had ceased,
And, with an agony subdued but passionately sad, a woman's sobbing!
Our eyes were wet, we could not think
But of ourselves were our dear ones to weep in vain for us—

A shout of boys, a whistle down the street;
A train loud hizzing with a flying steam;
A pat of footsteps in the silent night;
Whispers in shadows, women's voices once,
And in the end the lovely tolling of a single bell!

INDEX

About, Edmond, 71
Achiet - le - Petit, landscape round, 111
Architecture, beginning of Gothic, 31
Army, conditions in French, 44–45
Arras to Bapaume, road from, 62–64
Art, line and form in, 27–28
Attack, moving to the, 160–163

Barbizons, 19, 51
Barrage, artillery, 150–151
Battle-scenes, 147–150, 152–153
Bazin, René, 70
Beauty, the search after, 174–175
Belgium, battle in, 130–131
Belgium, shell-pitted horror of, 120
Black, William—
White Heather, 134
Boulogne, harbour of, 15–16
Boulogne to Etaples, march from, 16–17
Brangwyn, Frank, 160
Buchan, John—
Salute to Adventurers, 82
"Bull-Ring," 14

Camp, picturesque moments in Etaples, 7–8
Canal picture, 159
Christianity and the Crucifix, 78

Church, a country, 145–147
Civilization, peasant, 109–110
Cloud-pictures on battlefield, 88–89
Coleridge, S. T.—
Ancient Mariner, 132–133
Colour symphonies, 96–99
Conrad, Joseph—
Lord Jim, 34
Mirror of the Sea, 106
Cooper, Fenimore, 70
Corot, J. B. C., 28

Dante, 4, 10, 11, 33, 87, 95, 165
Daudet, Alphonse, 72
Dead at Ypres, pictures of the, 124–125
"Death and Glory," 12
Death, pictures of, 132
Denny Sadler, 23
De Quincey, 135
Desolation, hatred of, 113
Devieux, Henry, 144–145
Dickens, 70, 120
Dumas, Jr., Alexandre, 65, 83

Empire and Republic, 67–68
Epicurean philosophy, 107–108

Fampoux, incident at, 59
Fatigue, sensation of, 76–77
Fear, 123–124, 157–158
Flameng, François, 40

France, landscape of northern, 15
Fromentin, E., 72

German soldier, diary of, 99–101
Gissing, George—
 New Grub Street, 36–37
Glasgow, memories of, 135
Goethe—
 Wilhelm Meister, 36
Grimmelshausen—
 Simplicissimus, 83

Hardy, Thomas, 139
Hell's Fire Corner, 127–128
Hewlett, Maurice—
 Forest Folk, 140
 Open Country, 24.
Hospital, scenes in, 179–181

Inscriptions of French soldiers, 40

Knight, Laura, 90

Land divisions in France, 46
Landscape at Etaples, 4, 7, 13
Landscape by moonlight, 56–58
Landscape, pictorial elements in French, 28–30
La Rochefoucauld, 69
Lee, Vernon, 107, 108, 114
L'Hermitte, Tristan, 107

Malot, Hector, 70
Menin Road, 127, 170
Meredith, George, 24
Mist-pictures, 116–117
Morland, George, 49
Morris, William—
 The Well at the World's End, 129, 159
 The Wood Beyond the World, 85

Moselly—
 L'Aube Fraternelle, 182–183
Mud, 125–126
Mud, first acquaintance with, 22

Nicol, Erskine, 27
Night-march on the Somme, 74–77
Night-scene on the march, 53–54

Paris-Plage, 18
Pascal, 85–86
Passchendaele campaign, futility of, 176–179
Passchendaele, dramatic element in, 150–152
Pastoral scenes, 137–140, 164–165
Patrol incident, 120–122
Peasant, French, symbol of nature, 52
Popheringhe to Ypres, road from, 129

Rain, horror of, 163–164
Religion of the soldier, 183–186
Roberts, Morley—
 Henry Maitland, 36
Rosny, 70

St. Pol, 173
Sand, Georges, 71
Savy to Isel-le-Hameau, march from, 22–24
Savy, summer storm at, 19–21
School-books in ruined village, 65–66, 69–70
Shakespeare, 26, 84
Shelley, 94
Shop-signs in France, 41
Somerville and Ross—
 Some Irish Yesterdays, 85

INDEX

Somme, bombardment on, 91–93
Somme, German depredations in, 110
Somme, pictures of life in trenches at, 80–81
Speech, a war-, 118
Stoicism, 166
Storm at Isel-le-Hameau, 24–25
Swallow, incident of the, 73–74

Temple Thurston—
Richard Furlong, 29
Timothy, 58
Trenches at Ypres, life in, 122

Villon, François, 177

Vlamertinghe to Ypres, road from, 154–156

War, ethics of, 171–173
,, philosophy, of, 167–169
,, romance of, 104–105
,, tragedy of, 60–62, 141
Water-party, adventure of, 9–10
Webster, 27
Wells, H. G., 108
de Wint, Peter, 29

Ypres, 127–128
Ypres, battlefield of, 32–33
Ypres, canal-bank at, 153, 156–160

Zola, Émile, 15

Printed in Great Britain by
Amazon.co.uk, Ltd.,
Marston Gate.